My Sporting Icons

D1353828

My Sporting Icons

Colin Jackson

www.redshoesltd.com
2010

Royalties from this book will be donated to The Moses Project charity, established to develop an educational link between a Welsh community in the UK and a Maasai community in Kenya.

www.themosesproject.org.uk

My Sporting Icons by Colin Jackson

First published in Great Britain in 2010

by Red Shoes Productions Ltd

Copyright © 2010 Red Shoes Productions Ltd

The right of Colin Jackson and Red Shoes Productions Ltd to be identified as the author of this work has been asserted in accordance with the Copyright, Designs and Patents Act 1988.

All rights reserved. No part of this publication may be reproduced, stored in a retrieval system, or transmitted in any form or by any means, electronic, mechanical, photocopying, recording, or otherwise, without the prior permission of the copyright owner.

ISBN: 978-0-9567437-0-1

Cover design by
Jam Creative Studios

Front cover picture by
Sebastien LeClerc

Produced in Wales by
Keith Brown and Sons Ltd,
Cowbridge.

www.brownsprinters.co.uk

Contents

Hi there.

Not everyone has sporting icons. But I do!

The sporting icons I have chosen to include in this first book each, in their own way, represent aspects of greatness. Knowing them, in itself, was an experience which made me a better athlete – and a better person.

I always strove for perfection so I include David Hemery; Daley is here because he was the perfect package; Fatima is here for resilience; Steve Cram for sheer brilliance; Steve Backley for competitiveness. Each story illustrates an aspect of what is necessary to get to the top of your world. When you wonder how on earth to improve on a performance, whether it be in a sporting context or in a business or life situation – you may find the stories of these icons can inspire you to take a fresh look at your own situation.

Since retiring from track and field I have faced many new challenges which placed me firmly outside my comfort zone – take Strictly Come Dancing as just one example! The experiences of these iconic sporting people continue to motivate me to search for, and find, my own solutions – and I am grateful to them for sharing their stories, so honestly with me, for this book.

It's important to me that these friends tell their stories in their own words – not through a ghost writer or in a newspaper article, or in an edited piece of work. These personal stories are from their hearts – and I hope when you find something that catches your imagination, take that away and keep it with you.

For those who seek inspiration

Daley Thompson

"I wanted a lot out of it – so I decided to put the lot in."

We met in a small park on the banks of the river Thames, where I found Daley, ice cream cornet in one hand, signing autographs. I heard his laugh before I actually spotted his wide grin, and it took me back to the days when he was the one athlete I looked out for on TV. He looked like he enjoyed the decathlon, he looked like he enjoyed athletics, that was plain to see, and I wanted to be like him because I deduced that athletics must therefore be fun.

Daley was the epitome of the greatest athlete on the planet – and he himself would quite often assure people of that! I don't think anyone should curse him out for that either because if I had ever been as good as he was, then I would have been quite happy to tell everyone.

He is the King Midas of athletics. For him everything was about a bonus, so if you performed well, you should get something out of it. Forget about getting something for it before hand. I remember one time he showed me a pair of his cool black spikes and said that if I ran a certain time he would give me the spikes. Well I thought deep down that even if I didn't run the time he set me as a target, all I had to do was to come close to it, and he would surely give me the spikes. Well I didn't manage to run the time, even though I did come pretty close – but he didn't give me the spikes. Simple as that.

I bought my own ice cream and joined him on a bench, across the river from Fulham football stadium, and we watched the rowers passing up and down the river before us. It wasn't long before Daley gave in to the urge to shout to them.

DT: Come on put some effort into it, you should be sweating pints by now. That's where the Oxford Cambridge boat race starts over there by Putney Bridge. Did you know I went to boarding school? Not Oxford or Cambridge, mine was Farney Close Boarding School in Bolney in Sussex. Do you know of it Colin?

CJ: Afraid not no. Is that where you got into athletics?

DT: Yes it was, in the evenings because they saw I was so full of beans the teachers sent me down to the local athletics track to try and wear me out I guess! It was Haywards Heath Harriers club near Croyden and we used to train in the summer at a secondary school in Haywards Heath on a grass track. It had a couple of jumping pits and that kind of stuff and we just used to spend most of our time running around and acting the fool really! Looking back it was great to be out of doors and running around – it was a great habit to get into. If it wasn't for those teachers I sometimes wonder what I would have ended up doing with all the energy I had inside me!

CJ: So when did you decided to take things seriously?

DT: I don't recall that ever happening! I've never taken it too seriously! I used to go down to watch athletics at the West London Stadium and at Crystal Palace Stadium, which was great. You must have fun and at the start it was the most important thing for me. Then it became my business and I had to knuckle down and get on with the hard work, but I never thought about it really as a job. You don't suddenly decide to have fun, it just happens that way. You either enjoy the environment, the camaraderie and the total experience, or you don't, and I loved all of it and was enthralled by it all, so that meant I would enjoy getting into it and enjoy doing all of it, whether that be the preparation or the actual competing. These days with so much money at stake in sport some of the fun has gone out of it because people become more concerned with paying the mortgage and all that, and the pressure which that brings spills over and can consume all they do. You should worry about one thing at a time – or only worry about the things you can influence or change.

CJ: When did the fun stop for you then? I can't remember seeing you without a smile or a cheeky grin on your face!

DT: Well I don't think it ever stopped for me. I was ending my career when the big money came into it, so in a way money didn't threaten to spoil my enjoyment – not even the lack of money spoiled it for me! I am sure the audience saw that and recognised that in me. The danger these days is that if athletes are not having fun then people see their serious faces and don't empathise with them. They don't see or recognise enjoyment and often that means they won't like the way you play the game, and may not like you! Or worse still, not like the sport you play. It's true for any sport, the marketing starts with the way you play your game, the way you act and handle yourself in your arena, and these days with TV close ups people see inside the sport and the main characters represent the sport – and if they look miserable it doesn't reflect well on the sport. Kids, well not only kids but adults as well, are very impressionable, I imagine most people are looking for an enjoyable life outside whatever their nine to five job is, and if they see a sport that looks like fun, a sport that looks enjoyable, then they are more likely to want a bit of it, and want to go and watch, or even – God forbid – participate in it.

CJ: It must have been a nightmare for your competitors seeing you with a continuous smile on your face? There is nothing worse than being beaten by a rival with a big smile on his face!

DT: Well I always felt if I couldn't actually enjoy the decathlon competition, what was the point of spending three hundred and fifty days every year training for it! You can't train on Christmas day if you didn't like training.

CJ: I trained on Christmas day, and didn't eat Christmas dinner – but I can't imagine you missing Christmas dinner Daley!

DT: Colin yes I did train on Christmas day – in fact I trained twice on Christmas day, because I reckoned everyone else trained once that day! But I didn't say I ever skipped Christmas dinner!

CJ: No, I thought not. When I retired I can remember thinking, boy am I going to pig out on Christmas day, but you know what, when I did, I didn't really think I had missed out on much over all those years! Sorry Mum that is no reflection at all on your cooking by the way!

DT: No your Mum is a fine cook I can testify to that. I always felt that the easy bits were the day to day training and certainly competition day. The difficult bit was putting together a good long block of training, three or four months worth, where you have to stay mentally focussed and fresh for such a long time with no competing. That if anything was the bit I had to be aware of and take care over.

CJ: So training partners must have been really important?

DT: Absolutely Colin. The guys who are with you for those long periods of time are crucial. They were so important to me that I gave away all my gold medals to them. I had four or five people that I could train with most days. I certainly didn't need decathletes or people who were going to push me in any particular event. What I needed was great company. Even I who loved the event, could get bored and stale, so I needed companions to lighten the load. So even on the worst days, when for whatever reason, I didn't feel up to training, I would still be going off to 'meet up with the boys', and before I knew it I was into the training. To me that added up, so when I used to win – me giving them my medals went some way to show them just how much they meant to me.

CJ: Did you have to have a favourite event in the decathlon?

DT: Not really no. I liked them all. I had to make myself like them all because you can't hide from a certain part of the decathlon or it will find you out, and you would fold in a competition. So I used to make myself like them all, and in my mind I would look forward to each and every one of them, even the 1500m which I wasn't very good at, but I was happy to run it.

CJ: Now I found it hard to concentrate for my event which lasted thirteen seconds – how did you manage in a decathlon that lasted two days?

DT: Colin the secret is not to concentrate all of the time. Now I don't know if that sounds funny or off handish but it's not. It's a skill, being able to switch off say between jumps or throws and forget all about it, and then switch back on. You then look at it all from a brand new perspective, and that my friend was priceless.

CJ: You did whistle God Save the Queen on the podium once – were you switched off then?

DT: Hahaha, yes that . . . mmm . . . yes I did whistle it, and I enjoyed every moment of that ceremony, the flag going up the pole, the crowd, the anthem, the buzz of it all. You don't get many jobs where achievement is rewarded or appreciated quite like that. Although wouldn't it be great if one day you turned up to work at your office and your boss said well done Bob, fantastic piece of work Bob, and then proceeded to hoist the Union Jack and blast out the national anthem and have all the staff clap. What would that do for your morale!

CJ: Why did you whistle it?

DT: Have you heard my singing voice Colin?

CJ: Enough said. What about finishing day one with a hard 400m, and then starting day two with the 110m hurdles? I mean those hurdles are tough enough without hurting before you start!

DT: But the funny thing is that in fifteen years of being an international athlete I can count on one hand the number of times that I've felt sore. I prepared my body in training nearly every single day. The guys who were sore were the guys who didn't maybe train as hard as I did. Some people used to say that I made it look easy. Well the crucial part of that statement is the word 'look'. I worked tremendously hard to be in a position where I could then make it look easy.

CJ: What about the money in sport these days then, its inevitable isn't it that it changes the sport, for better or for worse?

DT: In athletics it's good that it's all above board now. My day was the era of the brown envelope under the table, so it's good that has changed. The fact that you can earn a living through athletics, well there's nothing bad in that, and if it's the attractive part to some people so be it. Yes athletics has changed beyond all recognition, and maybe is set to change again because at the moment we can't get enough kids into the sport, and that is true across many sports. All sports are suffering – except football it seems. There are so many other things that attract kids' attention like computer games and going to the movies, so all sports have to really think how to engage and attract kids. I mean all sports are up against the multi million pound marketing budgets of these computer games companies and such like, so it's a hard task. The sport and the people in the sport must make it attractive – and maybe that can start by them looking like they are having a good time. We also have to be willing to adapt the events to suit kids as spectators, that's why the new concepts of street athletics is great. We are missing the numbers coming into athletics, and participating at grass roots level. By having large numbers coming into the sport you will have more potential superstars on your hands.

CJ: Children can be drawn into a sport like say football, by the prospect of earning a lot of money from that particular sport?

DT: Well yes and we all need to work for a living, and that's why it's good that athletics is professional now. We can see Craven Cottage home to the mighty Fulham Football Club across the river there, the oldest professional football club in London and it's my favourite game – I still go down every couple of weeks. The general problem football has is that the guys who are not right at the top of the game are still paid huge amounts, which drains finances. It does not reflect well on the sport, and you can't buy loyalty. We need our top sports men and women to be role models. Not all kids will make it to the top of their sport, so we need role models to help turn out healthy kids, and I mean healthy in heart, mind and body.

CJ: You used to play a bit of football?

DT: Yes I did, not to anywhere near Fulham's standard though!

CJ: Really, you sure about that?

DT: Hey Fulham aren't that bad, we will rise again, but no I did play a bit for Mansfield . . . Stevenage Borough though and loved every moment of it.

CJ: So how do you keep in shape now then, because you are in shape!

DT: I always figured when I was in athletics that I trained as hard as I ever could so that gave me the right to eat what I liked! So for me it was hamburger and chips and all those things that I loved – paid for with an extra hour in the gym. These days I have to run around keeping up with the kids, and then I take on easier stuff like charity walks or cycle rides. I recently did London to Manchester on a bike, and I try and offer a bit of support to charities like the Rhys Daniels Trust. It's easy for me to do, and I try and make a small amount of difference.

CJ: You were undefeated for nine years, you won double Olympic Gold and countless other European, Commonwealth and World titles – is it a silly question to ask where your motivation and commitment came from?

DT: You are allowed to ask silly questions my friend! Motivation was never an issue for me, there were only one or two times a year when I didn't feel like training, so really that was not an issue. I was going to hang out with my mates doing the thing I loved the most, so I just thought to myself 'what else would I want to be doing!'

So far as commitment was concerned I didn't want for that either. In my mind commitment is going down a coal mine to earn your corn for your family. That's commitment. I wanted to get a lot out of the athletics route I was going down so I knew that I would only get out what I put in – so I put the lot in. But I often think, if I could somehow isolate what made me so committed and motivated, I would be a very rich man. And do you know what, I would buy Fulham Football Club and get them to the top of the Premiership. Now that would be a dream come true!

Daley Thompson CBE

Medals at major championships

Olympic Games

GOLD	1980	Moscow	Decathlon
GOLD	1984	Los Angeles	Decathlon

World Championships

GOLD	1983	Helsinki	Decathlon

European Championships

SILVER	1978	Prague	Decathlon
GOLD	1982	Athens	Decathlon
GOLD	1986	Stuttgart	Decathlon

Commonwealth Games for England

GOLD	1978	Edmonton	Decathlon
GOLD	1982	Brisbane	Decathlon
GOLD	1986	Edinburgh	Decathlon
SILVER	1986	Edinburgh	4 x 100m

Personal best

100m	10.26 sec	1986	Stuttgart
Long Jump	8.11m	1978	Edmonton
Shot Put	16.10m	1984	Walnut
High Jump	2.14m	1982	Amarillo
400m	46.86 sec	1982	Götzis
110mH	14.04 sec	1986	Stuttgart
Discus	49.10 m	1986	Stanford
Pole Vault	5.25 m	1986	London
Javelin	65.38 m	1980	Götzis
1500m	4.20.3 sec	1976	Cwmbran
Total	9315		

b. 30th July 1958. Notting Hill, London.

Daley had three fierce rivals Guido Kratschmer, Jürgen Hingsen and Siggy Wentz, all of whom were German, and despite him being smaller than them, Daley took the decathlon event to new heights of popularity and profile – by winning, with a smile on his face.

Daley showed early promise and set three World Junior records, and in 1977 won gold at the European Junior Championships in the decathlon. Who should be close behind him in third place that day but his arch rival of the future Jürgen Hingsen. Daley also placed fifth in the individual long jump competition at those championships.

Daley's first Olympic Games were in 1976 in Montreal. He was 18 years old. He finished 18th! Yet only four years later he won the gold medal at the 1980 Moscow Olympics, finishing 150 points ahead of his nearest rival. He went on to retain his Olympic title in 1984 in Los Angeles with Jurgen Hingsen in second place. During his career Daley broke the world record for the decathlon four times and went undefeated in all competitions for nine years between 1979 and 1987. He also gained Commonwealth silver at the 4 x 100m relay and finished sixth in the individual pole vault event at the Edinburgh Games of 1986!

He began the 1980 season with a world decathlon record of 8,648 points at Götzis, Austria, and followed this with his first gold medal win at the Moscow Olympics. In 1982 again in Götzis, Austria he raised the world record to 8,730 points. The 1982 European Championships in Athens, was an almighty showdown with Hingsen that saw Daley winning gold with a new world record points total of 8,774. Thanks to Daley the decathlon event was now attracting far more interest than it ever had before.

In 1983 Daley took his success to new heights as he became the inaugural World Champion, beating Hingsen, who was by then the world record holder, and Siefried Wentz. Daley became the first decathlete to hold the European, World and Olympic titles simultaneously.

By the time the 1984 Olympics came around Jürgen Hingsen had captured the world record from Daley, lost it, and recaptured it again, and so the showdown was set up. Daley was supreme, and the result was a repeat of the World Championships with Hingsen and Wentz in second and third. His long jump mark would have placed him fifth overall in the individual event! In the 1500m he tired coming up the home straight and missed the world points record by just a single point. However a year later he was awarded the record since when the photo finish pictures of the 110mH race were examined, it was seen he should have been awarded one extra point. So Daley was announced as joint world record holder which, when the scoring was recalculated under the newly introduced scoring table, made him sole world record holder with 8,847 points, a mark that stood until 1992.

Daley's rivalry with the German decathletes, especially the 2m tall Hingsen, is legendary, and what has come to be known as the finest decathlon competition of all time came at the 1986 European Championships in Stuttgart. Hingsen and Wentz were battling Daley in their own backyard, and as the competition went on the German crowd booed Thompson relentlessly. Hingsen at one stage offered his apologies to Daley for the crowd's behaviour, and at the end of a momentous competition Daley took the Gold. He then paraded around the stadium wearing a T-shirt saying "Bernhard, Boris and Daley, Germany's favourite sons" as a light hearted repost referring to golfer Bernhard Langer, tennis player Boris Becker – and Daley himself. The home crowd didn't find it quite as hilarious as Daley obviously did.

Allan Wells

"Down, crouch and go!"

As I drove up to the Surrey University campus, Allan was waiting outside the entrance for me. He was easy to spot even from a distance – because of his shape. Shortish, squattish, thickish set with still a hint of the thin athletic waist and block like thighs only sprinters and cyclists can own!

Allan always seemed like a grafter to me, and when someone works as hard as he did, then they deserve their just rewards. Similar to all of my icons in this book, Allan's dreams really did come true. For me he was a role model – in that if you work hard, you can succeed. We were never in the same British team, so he was someone I watched from a distance mainly on the telly. He was the first Brit to have head to head races and take on the Americans – and beat them at their own game. He was also sprinting and competing at an age which was seen as being quite old for a sprinter – so in a way he proved that with age comes a maturity, and that if you can use that, you can still be more than competitive against the cocky young whipper snappers coming into the sport.

We sat surrounded by lush Surrey countryside, and as our chat went on, his Scottish accent definitely got stronger with the passion of his storytelling. When we finished we were both wet, yet neither of us seemed to have noticed when the rain had come down?

I came to a definite conclusion: Allan Wells loves sprinting.

CJ: Here we are in Surrey University near Guilford, what do you do here Allan?

AW: Well quite a number of things to do with the new leisure complex here, and I also work as a systems engineer and do some project management which all keeps me pretty busy. I also look after a few athletes and mentor some Scottish athletes so there's always something going on. Busy busy!

CJ: Can I take you way, way back in time Allan, to the start of the journey that led to your dreams coming true?

AW: Yes, you can't put it any other way really, my dreams did come true. I was actually born on a council estate, 100m from an athletics track, yes really! We lived in Fernieside Crescent on the south side of Edinburgh. It was really quite appropriate and that definitely gave me my early inspiration to be honest. I used to go down as a wee boy and watch all the athletes training on that track. The jumpers, the throwers and the distance runners they all intrigued me, but it was the sprinters that really captured my imagination. I remember getting shouted at because I used to run with the sprinters. Well when I say run with them, I mean they would be on the track and I would be running on the rough ground the other side of the stadium fence. I was very young and they soon told me in no uncertain terms to 'clear off'. That whole period was an inspiration for me. Then later on in life I would watch the athletics when it was on the telly, and I can remember watching Lynn Davies, who won Olympic Gold in the long jump. For me he depicted the perfect athlete, I mean he combed his hair perfectly before every jump! He was tall, handsome just like a film star really! But seriously he did look the part and was a great athlete and I really looked up to him. My first club was Edinburgh Southern Harriers, and I went along there with my friend Chris Black, who lived a few doors away from me, and that's how it all started. Chris went on to win nine Scottish hammer throwing titles and went to two Olympics himself.

CJ: I think I read somewhere that you raked the sand pit at the 1970 Commonwealth Games just to get a closer look at Lynn. Did you then begin to dream??

AW: Ha ha ha you are making me sound like Lynn's stalker!! I think I did dream of such things, what young boy or girl doesn't dream of achieving something in life, whether that's in sport or not, but to be honest it's what stands between a dream and reality which is the big part that defeats so many. Getting that right is the beauty of the achievement, and at that stage in life, understandably, you don't fully appreciate that bit I guess.

CJ: In my childhood, when I was 14 or 15, I remember that you were the athlete who never used starting blocks – even in top class and international meets, while everyone else did. Wow!

AW: Yes, unfortunately I think it was a wee bit lazy of me! I mean all athletes had to carry their own blocks to the start of the race, so by the time I arrived there my shoulders would be hanging off from lugging these cumbersome contraptions! So I thought to heck with that! But the way our group trained involved a heck of a lot of starts, and using blocks would have meant continuously moving them for others to have their go in the lane, so it was far quicker, or more convenient just to use marks and not blocks. That way you were down and away quickly, and the next person could step into the lane and do the same. Down, crouch and go!! Down, crouch and go! That brings back memories, if I had a pound for every time I practised that – but anyway less of those thoughts Colin! However I don't think the IAAF liked seeing me starting without blocks, so they made them compulsory! My claim to fame!

CJ: Did you get used to them quickly?

AW: Well I had to, but it was more of a progression thing for me. I was 'enthusiastic and semi professional' in my approach, and as I got better and better, I found I didn't quite have the system or the same backup behind me as many other athletes had. We had converted a garage to use as a gym, and that's where I used to do hours and hours on the speedball and the weights and do mini circuits in there. Pretty humble stuff, and I know Colin you would agree with me on this because I have heard you say it too, if you have a chip on your shoulder it certainly can help you succeed in sport. You want to be a winner so bad, it helps, and that's how it was for me.

CJ: The boycott of the Moscow Olympics by quite a few countries including the Americans – did that affect your event?

AW: Well first of all we weren't sure for ages if we as a team were going or not. I think eventually despite huge pressure from the British Government the British Olympic Organisation decided to send the team. I was struggling with a back injury so I was oblivious to it all trying to get into shape. The American's did not go so two of my rivals in the 100m were absent, Mel Lattany and Stanley Floyd, and Stanley was the fastest man in the world that year and was totally world class as well!

CJ: Well your time to deliver, came in the 1980 Moscow Olympics and the 100m event first of all. What was going on in your mind!

AW: Well In Moscow, in the 100m, the second round was the interesting thing, because that race had five world class athletes going for three guaranteed places in the semi final, as well as one fastest loser place. It was crazy! It included the reigning Olympic Champion Hasley Crawford of Trinidad as well as Pietro Mennea the Italian world record holder for the 200m, and he was the fastest white man at that time, and there was the European Champion . . . so I had to go out there and face them all.

CJ: Now I remember your wife being ever present by your side in those days.

AW: Yes indeed and Margot was a wee bit worried and anxious to say the least – as were the team management – that this was such a loaded heat. There was no use complaining about it. What could you do? I mean if a referee blows for a penalty he doesn't change his mind does he. It was a case of me having to say to myself 'I must win this race'. I can't change the way the heats worked out, and this is what I face, so get on with it. Simple as that, but it was an awesome line up.

CJ: Simple as that – win the race!?

AW: Yes! Simple as that! I had to go out and give, if not 100% certainly 99% you know Colin. It was a wee bit psychological and it does take a lot out of you mentally just to make sure you are not worrying about who you are racing. It certainly focuses the mind when you are in a situation of facing those guys – just to make the semi final. There could be no mistakes. Any mistake and my dream would have been over, and the records would show I was elininated in the heats!

CJ: So how did you fare?

AW: Well I won the race! Simple as that – if only! It was a new British record time of 10.11s, and I was easing up a little at the line so I could have gone close to 10.0 something. But it felt more like a final, it was just as intense as many finals I had run! However I think Margot was more relieved than I was! I guess when you get to the Olympic Games you will have to beat the best at some stage, and you hope that one race will be the final, so to do that in the heat was an achievement in itself, and I picked myself up and got through the semi final.

CJ: And just when you were patting yourself on the back after the heats and the semi final, you find yourself preparing, at last, for the Olympic final – although you must have felt like you had run it already!

AW: Well it did feel a little like 'right what mountain next!' You had people like the great Don Quarrie going out at the semi final stage – so that shows you how ferocious the competition was. But the gauge for me in the final was a sprinter called Silvio Leonard of Cuba, who was in lane 1. Silvio was the second fastest man on earth at that time, and he had run 9.98s in 1977. We couldn't have been further apart as I was in lane 8, so I couldn't really keep an eye on him he was too far away. His team mate Osvaldo Lara was in lane 7 next to me, and I had watched them training and knew that Silvio Leonard would be a yard up on Lara after 30m, so that would give me some idea of where I was in the race, and that was my strategy. Unfortunately it took me till 30 or 40m to get past Lara and I was only a yard past him after 50m so I was thinking where on earth Leonard was by that stage! So I knew I faced an enormous last part of the race. I think it was only the depth of my wanting to win that took me through to the tape, and to be on the line neck and neck with Leonard. I remember dipping for the line like I had never dipped before and afterwards no one really knew who had won it. I did feel like I had it, and I won it by the thickness of my vest as they say.

CJ: It was close but not quite a dead heat!

AW: No not quite, we were given the same time of 10.25s but the photo finish gave me a 3 inch lead. It was the dip at the end that won it for me.

CJ: Did it feel like what you expected it to feel like?

AW: Well I didn't really know what to expect it to feel like Colin. It was a huge experience of relief, and huge satisfaction, as you know Colin when you work that hard at something and you come through the other end and get success, especially at that sort of level, you know it is a huge reward. I knew that despite the boycott I had come up against the best sprinters in the world, and had taken them on in the heat, the semi final and the final.

CJ: Taken them on and beaten them! Was Margot pleased?

AW: Margot was indeed pleased!

CJ: So you were crowned Olympic Champion of the 100m – but that was one down and one to go, because you had the task of doubling up in the 200m.

AW: Aye and that proved to be as difficult a task as I imagined it would be. When you are in that situation you do need a lot of support people behind you, to help you, and I didn't really have that. But I was focussed and I was determined. I can remember I wasn't getting much sleep at all at night out there, only about 4 hours a night. I don't know why. I was rooming with Sebastian Coe, but I was like semi conscious during the night. It was terrible! I've never told anyone but I did have a bottle of Georgian wine which someone had given me. Now I didn't drink, but because I was so tired I decided I had to do something to try and get a decent night's sleep. So the night before the 200m final I took out the bottle of wine and took it round and offered a glass to some others in the accommodation – but there were no takers, so by the time I got back to my room, it turned out I drunk the whole bottle myself! On top of that I found a bottle of beer, so that went down as well, and by then the room was spinning round and round. I didn't know where I was, but I was determined to get a good night sleep. Anyway I was out like a light, fully clothed I think Colin! But horror of horrors four hours later, I woke up and was wide awake again! I just could not believe it; I was sober as a judge, wide awake and very tired.

CJ: Goodness so what shape were you in at the blocks of the 200m final?

AW: Well sleep was a really important part of my life as an athlete, it was one of the ingredients that enabled me to run fast and deliver when it really mattered. So not being able to sleep really was an issue for me and that's why I did what I did the night before. But it didn't work for me, and it was going to be so hard having tasted the elation of winning one Gold medal, having to go out there feeling tired to try to win a second gold medal. I remember there was a false start, not by me I might add, and as I walked back to my blocks I thought to myself 'hey wake up this is the only chance you will have in your lifetime to win two Olympic gold medals'. I can remember it quite clearly, and it was at that split second that I realised just how badly I wanted to win that second title. But it was a difficult task since I was running against people who could run faster than me – on paper! So I sort of shook myself and said OK I am going to give it all I've got – and more.

CJ: Thank heavens for false starts eh!

AW: Indeed! I had Pietro Mennea the world record holder in lane 8, I was next to him in lane 7, and I knew Mennea was going to come through and attack me at the end, and that he would get onto my shoulder maybe in the last 50m and try and go through. The gun went and I am on the inside of him so I have got to do my own thing, I can't wait for him, so I am flying round the bend, eating up the stagger, pounding that bend, I was flying. Now with 50m to go, he wasn't there. 30m to go and he still wasn't there. So I am thinking where the heck is Mennea? Well he finally turns up on my shoulder with 15m to go. I still managed to react to him, I still pulled something out from deep inside somewhere, but it was just too late. Just a little too late. I even thought he might have made a mistake by easing up just before the line, and that I had a chance in the final yard or two to get ahead of him, but no. He won it.

CJ: It was that close again, he beat you by 0.02s!

AW: It was close yes, but, Colin, as they say, I left it all out there on the track, and my time was 20.21s so I have no complaints. It was pretty quick so I could not have come any closer to winning the double.

CJ: And that timing was a new British record.

AW: It was aye, and afterwards Pietro Mennea's Mum was quoted as saying 'my son beat the big bull'. Now I am not sure which part of a big bull I resemble, and I haven't pursued the matter with her since, but suffice to say that I think Mennea deserved it. He was the better man on the day, but I settled for my Gold and Silver medals because look I had beaten the great Don Quarrie and Silvio Leonard again, and they were all faster than me – on paper. As you know Colin when you beat guys that are faster than you on paper, what it takes to do that can give you enormous satisfaction. Even though I didn't win the race outright, it did make me even more aware of what I was capable of when you forget what was written down on paper and you just lined up against each other. Man against man. Human against human if you like.

CJ: Did you feel that your achievements in Moscow were somewhat overshadowed by the Coe and Ovett rivalry, and their races in the 800 metres and the 1500 metres?

AW: Mmm . . . an interesting question Colin. When I look back at it now, no I don't. It's a different event, and has got a different following. I am not going to say that the 100 metres is the blue riband event, but I think a lot of people outside Britain think it's definitely the blue riband event. I was the first Briton since 1924 to win the Olympic title, it was the closest 100m final at the Olympics for 28 years, so it was a top quality competition and might I say worthy of a great Olympic sprint final. In Britain there was a lot of interest in the all British clash in the middle distance events between Coe and Ovett, but I think people's reactions to me were that they all watched the 100m as well as the middle distance events. But the point is we were focussed on our own thing, and I never thought about what the public were thinking or watching at home, and to win Olympic Gold in those days, well, it really was a big deal. As you would know yourself Colin – or rather as you would not know!

CJ: Quite right Allan, silver was the best I could manage. Well you are the best judge of the scale of the achievements in Moscow because you were sharing a room with Seb Coe right?

AW: Yes I was and I will share a story with you. I remember Peter Coe, Seb's father and coach coming into our room and picking up my Gold medal in his hand, and examining it closely, almost lovingly. He then turned to Seb and said 'that is the only colour of medal we want to leave with', and you know I think that gave Seb an extra edge, only a slight one maybe, but in sport slight edges make a huge difference.

CJ: I read somewhere that Seb Coe was so nervous and his hands were shaking so much that he couldn't stir his tea the morning of his final?

AW: Well it's a long time ago for me to remember that detail Colin, but it is a nice picture to imagine. I don't recall that Seb took sugar, although that doesn't mean he didn't still stir his tea – I guess that is an English thing right!?

CJ: Quite possibly, but your room must have been like a pressure cooker!

AW: In a way yes! I think, my Gold medal being in his, or our room gave him that edge, and to be honest looking back at it now, it may have taken a slight edge away from me to win the 200m. I am not saying I was complacent but when you have won an Olympic Gold, well, you have won an Olympic Gold! To win two is on another level, almost beyond your dreams, beyond your wildest dreams, and to prepare for that and execute it was new territory, certainly psychologically for me, as it would have been for most people. I mean that was the plan for both Coe and Ovett, to win the double in the middle distance events, and look how that turned out for both of them – but that as well was great drama.

I came close, as I say I couldn't have come closer, but when the curtain came down I had gold and silver, and as you can imagine from your own experiences Colin – I was happy with that and had I known that, a few years earlier, in the garage doing my weights, I think I would have settled for that!

CJ: When did you next race the Americans that weren't in Moscow due to the boycott?

AW: Two weeks after the Olympics! I could and should have been back at home resting my back, but I guess I was aware that they had not been in Moscow, so there was a score to settle, or a question to put to bed. So at an athletics meet in Lobenz, Germany, I lined up against Lattany and Floyd. I was putting my head in a noose really, it was a no win situation in many respects. But you know me Colin, in at the deep end, see what comes out the other side!

CJ: Now that sounds interesting! I remember doing something similar after the Barcelona Olympics, but I had lost the final, and had something to prove in the races that followed. You were putting the credibility of your titles on the line?

AW: Well it was a big ask for me, especially that soon after the Olympics, because I was absolutely drained! I only made the 100m final as the slowest qualifier. It was dreadful, I remember lying around before the final thinking I have no energy, and the one thing I could not do Colin?

CJ: Pull out!

AW: Absolutely! In for a penny in for a pound, I could not pull out. That would have been worse than losing against them. Mel Lattany and Stanley Floyd were fresh and they were up for it, and they couldn't wait to prove a point and dethrone the Olympic Champion! But you know Colin, the beauty of athletics – and this is why I had success in my career – is that it comes down to what happens on the track not off it. Somehow I was mentally strong enough to make sure that anything that happened before the gun or after the tape, did not matter. It did not affect me. Between gun and tape it's up to me, and I could be in control of that. But I don't know how deep I had to dig that night, but it was pretty deep, and I think I again surprised myself, because I tore them up and beat them all. That moment was nearly as good a feeling as winning the title in Moscow!

CJ: Well I think that is the sign of a true champion, the pressure, the intense pressure and you still delivered. It goes your way. Pure class.

AW: Mel Lattany came up to me afterwards, shook my hand, and said that he was really pleased for me, he had been trying to beat Floyd for the last eighteen months and couldn't. He did actually say that even if the two of them had been at Moscow he reckoned I would still have taken the Olympic title – and I thought that was very gracious of him. I will always remember that.

CJ: Do you still watch athletics; do you still get excited about the sprints?

AW: Yes I do watch it partly to see the physical side but also to see how people react psychologically. I also want to hear what you and Jonathan Edwards and Steve Cram have to say! I can then criticise you all. Joking! But as you can imagine I have my opinions. I like to see the sprinters before they race because in the middle distances you can run tactically. In the sprints you have to be flat out from the start. There may be some element of tactics, but generally it was gun to tape stuff, flat out, not holding anything back. That's how I ran. And before the race getting in the zone is a skill, which some spectators can misread for arrogance.

CJ: Do you think it's possible to psyche out a world class athlete?

AW: Yes! In some ways we thought the Russian was doing it in Moscow in the final. I am telling you now he was late getting to the holding pen, which is where you gather before going out on the track. So in he comes, late, and all he was wearing was a pair of socks!

CJ: Good grief!

AW: Well ok a pair of socks – and pants – but no track suit, or shorts or vest or nothing. We noticed that he had blood trickling down from just below his pants. Now it might sound a bit gruesome, but you naturally take notice, and you look, and you think what the heck is going on here?! Has he had an injection? You get all agitated and your brain and your imagination go wild. I had someone come over to me and said 'Do you see that, do you see that?!' Well I was thinking 'yes I can see that!' All I could say to him was 'look, focus on your own race mate, don't let it disturb your own preparation, and don't, don't, don't let him, beat you, today'. I couldn't say anything else because that was what I had already decided to do myself. Colin the psychology of athletics excites me, I mean every time you go into a race you are putting yourself into the deep end, mentally, and it's what emerges out of the deep end, at the end of the race that matters. That's what I loved, and ok it may have been a bit masochistic, but I think the mental side is the most important side. I think I was blessed with the attitude, the discipline and the commitment to keep training. It was every day, and I took the line that if I hurt myself in the gym, then that gave me the confidence when I lined up for a race, that I had already established a benchmark of how much I could hurt myself and how far I could take my body. Hey, that's why I am sitting here with a sore back, a knee problem, a stiff elbow, a sore neck . . . but I know one thing – I count myself very fortunate to have achieved what I did.

CJ: Yes the training was certainly relentless! Would you like to coach Usain Bolt?

AW: Is that a job offer?! Then I will take it. Thank you. Hahaha. Coach Usain Bolt? Now that would be easy! I think Usain could be coached by half a dozen of the world's top class coaches and he would still be the same athlete. He is unique. He is so unique. He is so . . . uhhmm . . . different, it's almost indescribable. You just have to sit back and applaud him and praise him. He is 6ft 5" of natural ability and he loves running fast. It is a fantastic feeling to have and a fantastic thing to be able to watch! I mean, I loved it, I loved coming off that bend, you were flying, it felt like flying – and to imagine being 5 or 10 yards faster, like he is, it's phenomenal.

It's not even like driving a Ferrari. You are the human Ferrari! You are the engine, and you are the power. As a human being to be able to run fast, it is a phenomenal thing. I really am lost for words to describe it. I felt like that when I ran. I absolutely loved it. I really did.

CJ: I know, I can tell, I love it. Crikey, when did it start raining?

AW: I have no idea! Race you to the car. Down, crouch and go!

CJ: Hang on I wasn't ready . . . .

Allan Wells MBE

Medals at major championships

Olympic Games

GOLD	1980	Moscow	100m
SILVER	1980	Moscow	200m

European Cup

GOLD	1979	Turin	200m
GOLD	1981	Zagreb	100m
GOLD	1983	London	200m
SILVER	1981	Zagreb	200m
SILVER	1983	London	100m
BRONZE	1979	Turin	100m

Commonwealth Games for Scotland

GOLD	1978	Edmonton	200m
GOLD	1978	Edmonton	4 x 100m
GOLD	1982	Brisbane	100m
GOLD	1982	Brisbane	200m
SILVER	1978	Edmonton	100m

Personal best

100m	10.11 sec	1980	Moscow
200m	20.21 sec	1980	Moscow

both are still Scottish records

b. 3rd May 1952. Edinburgh, Scotland.

Allan began his athletic career as a jumper, and won the Scottish Junior triple jump title. He also won the Scottish indoor long jump title in 1974, but his later sprinting achievements define him as an athlete – although it took him until 1976 to achieve a legal clocking of better than 11.0s for the 100m. His improvement rapidly continued as he won the AAA Indoor 60 metres title in 1977.

In July 1978, Allan equalled Peter Radford's 20-year-old UK 100 metres record of 10.29s and within a week he brought the record down to 10.15s. The same year at the Commonwealth Games in Edmonton he set a UK record of 20.61s in his heat of the 200m, before running a wind-assisted 20.12s to win the final. In the 100m he pushed Jamaican legend Don Quarrie all the way but was edged into second place by 0.04s. He did complete a double gold performance though, as part of an outstanding performance from the winning Scottish 4 x 100m relay team. Allan returned home having really announced his arrival to British athletics fans, as a serious medal contender on any stage.

In 1979, he twice improved the British 200m record and defeated Pietro Mennea, Italy's new World Record holder over 200m at the European Cup on Mennea's home territory in Turin. Allan also won bronze in the 100m.

1980 was Olympic year yet 65 countries boycotted the Games in protest over Russia's invasion of Afghanistan. The British Olympic Association went against the British Government's call to join the boycott, and so Allan went to Moscow, watched by a public who had understandable expectations that he could take on the best.

He was the 100m and 200m British record holder, and began well as he set a new UK record of 10.11s in the heats of the 100 metres. He went on to win a desperately close final – both he and the pre-race favourite, Silvio Leonard of Cuba, were given the same electronic time of 10.25s but it was Allan, at the age of 28, who became the oldest ever winner of the Olympic 100m title, on a photo finish. He failed by the narrowest of margins to win the 200m although his time of 20.21s, behind Mennea, was a new British record. He claimed a third British record as a member of the relay team that finished in fourth place in 38.62s.

He went on to race against the top Americans who had missed the Moscow Olympic Games, and beat them. In 1981, after a successful tour of Australia and New Zealand, Allan won the European Cup 100m, beating East German Frank Emmelmann, and finished with silver in the 200m.

He then demonstrated his calibre by finishing first in the "IAAF Golden Sprints" in Berlin; which was the most prominent sprint meeting in the world that year. Although defeated by the Frenchman Hermann Panzo in the 100m, Allan dominated the top four American sprinters Mel Lattany, Jeff Phillips, Stanley Floyd and Steve Williams as well as Canada's Ben Johnson in the 100m and 200m, winning the overall event on aggregate.

With his wins at the World Cup and the European Cup in 1981, Allan confirmed his position at the top of world sprinting. In October at the 1982 Commonwealth Games in Brisbane he won the 100 metres title in a time of 10.02s beating Canada's Ben Johnson into second. In the 200 metres final not even the photo finish could separate first and second so he shared the title, on a dead heat, with England's Mike McFarlane.

He lost out on medals at the 1983 World Championships finishing fourth in both the 100m and 200m, in races that were dominated by the American sprinters.

In 1984, at 32, he made the British Olympic team for a second time but was eliminated in the semi-finals of the 100m.

Allan lives in Surrey with wife Margot, works at Surrey University, and is still involved in the development of young sprinters.

Jonathan Edwards

"Run fast and jump far. It's as easy as shelling peas."

On the way up to Newcastle to meet up with Jonathan I stopped off at the roadside to take a look at the 'Angel of the North.' I have passed it quite a few times on my travels, but I have never really bothered to take a closer look. The first thing that struck me was that close up its much, much bigger than you originally think. It's a formidable icon that is by now easily identifiable with the North East. Jonathan Edwards fits that bill too. He will forgive me for saying that at best – he looked frail! Like we say in Wales – he hadn't been eating all his greens. But up close – he was a formidable competitor, and he brought his event to the attention of the public in a way that no-one previously had done.

He is a buddy, a work colleague and his athletic journey coincided with mine. He was a little un, who took it to the big uns and really socked it to them, and for that I have real admiration for him. Triple jump is all about power, but he was so graceful he made it look easy. In the 1999 World Championships in Seville I had won my second world title and I was on my lap of honour, and he was on the triple jump runway and I caught his eye and clenched my fist in encouragement and shouted 'come on do it'. He finished third, and I was really disappointed for him, and it slightly took the edge off my win.

He is the only person I know, who made a career out of hop-scotch!

He had invited me to do a bit of cycling with him, whilst we chatted, but I didn't fancy cycling the busy streets of Newcastle – so I turned up in jeans much to his annoyance as he opened his front door. Well I didn't know the North East had wide open countryside did I!

JE: You've not got your cycling gear on?

CJ: Good morning, how are you, a coffee would be good mate. Listen I haven't ridden a bike for years.

JE: Well it's never too late in life Colin.

CJ: Yea yea. So how much time do you spend mountain biking?

JE: Not enough. I can get out in the countryside around Newcastle and keep fit, because I don't like running because you don't get much aerobic fitness training for the triple jump, so I've never done much running. I don't want to go to the gym, so I get out on the bike. It's a way of having fun because keeping fit for fit's sake just doesn't inspire me. Let's have a chat out on the common behind the house, you can see the whole of Newcastle from there. Take that spare bike.

CJ: It took you quite a long time to be inspired to win your first major championship title!

JE: Very funny – hey I was inspired but I just couldn't quite get there. I was a late starter and I wonder if I would ever emerge if I was starting out in athletics nowadays. Everyone is getting younger and being lottery funded from a young age. I often wonder whether I would have had the self belief to keep hacking away on the road to being a major champion.

CJ: How late a starter were you?

JE: I was 21 years old when I left University and decided to give athletics a go. I had never got a junior international vest, and I was never a world junior champion like you were and progressing through from an early age. When I went to the Olympics in 1988 I was 22 years old and that was my very first representative honour for my country.

CJ: Don't tell me that was your first time away from home on an athletics trip?

JE: Not quite, I had been to the World Student Games the year before in Zagreb, where I finished ninth!

CJ: Is that last?

JE: Shut it! The guy who won that was Kenny Harrison who beat me in the 1996 Olympics in Atlanta. Funny how I kept bumping into the same old faces and they kept beating me!

CJ: I really understand that feeling, it's awful – but revenge can be sweet! So when you went to the World Championships in Gothenburg in 1995, which I want to talk about later – how old were you then?

JE: I was 29 years old then!

CJ: Wow! What sort of environment did you exist in?

JE: When I started out in athletics it was all tied up with my Christian faith and that was what I thought God wanted me to do. So to be honest, initially, it was nothing more than that. When I first moved up here to Newcastle I signed on the dole, I claimed housing benefit and it was a very humble beginning. My lifestyle was one many people would recognise, I just remember trying to feed myself in my bedsit, look after myself. Look down there, over there in the distance, you can just see the Royal Victoria Infirmary in Newcastle. That's where I had my first job in a laboratory there. It was a normal nine to five job, and after work I would then get a lift to Gateshead stadium, train as best I knew how there, and get the bus back and arrive home about 9pm. Then try and cook myself a meal in my flat, or get a take away and stick the telly on. It was quite a normal everyday existence really, and one many hopeful teenage athletes would recognise. Only I was 21 years old. I would not quite have believed then that it would all end up quite how it did.

CJ: What kept you going from 21 to 29 years old?

JE: Well once I made the decision to give athletics a go, I did make pretty reasonable progression each year; 1988 I was at the Olympics; 1989 I jumped 17m for the first time; 1990 I got a Commonwealth silver medal; 1991 I nearly jumped 17.50m; 1992 I won the World Cup; 1993 I got a bronze at the World

Championships; 1994 another Commonwealth silver so there was always something to keep me going. But I also had, deep down, and I don't really know where it came from, a belief that I could do something really special, and that I had this talent inside that hadn't really expressed itself fully.

CJ: What was it like waiting for that to happen because you were still 'on the undercard' to me and Sally Gunnell, and Linford Christie and quite a few others who were delivering at major championships.

JE: It was very difficult, but most great athletes are full of self belief. Whilst they will say they are full of doubts – as I did just before I competed – if you get right to the core of you there is something that says 'I can achieve something and the potential inside hasn't been fulfilled yet', and looking back I had that, and I realise now that is really important.

CJ: What were those times like?

JE: Well I will tell you a story, I remember going to a little athletic meet I think it was in Vigo, Port of Spain, where I jumped 17m 7cm, gale assisted, and I was there with Liz McColgan's husband Peter McColgan. Now afterwards everyone was queuing up outside the treasurer's hotel room to get their money. Well Peter and I looked at each other wondering 'do we get any money?' So we hesitantly joined the queue not having a clue whether we would be getting anything, and the big stars were coming out of the room with thick wads of cash, and when we reached the front of the queue we said 'We are Jonathan Edwards and Peter McColgan – have we got any money? Do we . . . do you think . . . any chance . . . ' and if they had said no, then we would have quite happily walked out and gone home! I think we were given about $200.

CJ: Was it quite daunting going through all that?

JE: Daunting? It was a nightmare! It's not like that now with agents and bank transfers and all that, but back then, well, it was like 2am queuing outside the treasurer's room, it was bizarre. So there must have been a belief in myself for me to do that, because there are so many people around you making sacrifices for your fledgling career, if you didn't really believe you could do it you wouldn't put them through that would you! With hindsight I look back and I begin to realise just how focussed and driven I was, because there's no way you just bumble along through athletics thinking 'well I am just some normal guy, and what will be will be.' So when I do look back I realise just how . . . neurotic and paranoid and kind of on the edge of normality I was as an elite athlete. It is frightening because to anyone looking in on that existence it cannot make much sense? As an athlete you go through so much disappointment that if you didn't have that mentality, then you just wouldn't do it. You just would not do it! Also those disappointments are shared for others around you, and that, as well as the overwhelming sense of letting them down consumes many athletes – but the best just don't let that distract them from the goal. Crickey I am making it sound so hard, it's enough to put everyone off!

CJ: If it was easy everyone would achieve it. I empathise with that, you become so extreme that it comes across as you being the most selfish person ever. I see photos of me – especially during one particular period of my track life – and I look anorexic. And yet without that selfish determination and sole purpose attitude – I certainly don't think I could have done what I did. Since retiring I have met many people, outside athletics, outside sport, who have that and have succeeded in other aspects of life – in business for example.

JE: Well take 1994 which was a really hard time for me, I trained so hard that winter, too hard as it turned out. I didn't listen to my body – maybe I didn't quite know or fully understand how to do that. But I took it past the extreme level into dangerous territory. I had a virus and I continued to train through it and I drove myself practically to a state of physical depression. That season turned out to be a disaster for me, and I ended up sixth in the European Championships.

CJ: What was the urge to train so hard?

JE: I mistakenly thought that the harder I trained the further I could jump, and I learnt that for me that wasn't the way it worked. My body and mind doesn't work like that; there are other vitally important factors that enable me to jump further that are not connected with how hard I trained.

CJ: Was it you taking that decision to train or the people around you?

JE: Honestly a bit of both but ultimately the decision was driven by me. It's a lesson you learn as an athlete and I learnt it the hard way, and I decided after that that I would only have to learn that lesson once!

CJ: Were there local heroes in this area who you looked up to in particular?

JE: Well on leaving Durham University the attraction of coming to train at Gateshead was that it is seen as one of the homes of British athletics, and certainly Brendan Foster made it that. I met Brendan fairly early after moving here and he was always very supportive. In 1993 I think, he gave me a grant out of the Great North Run Foundation which helped me focus and apply more time to my athletics. I remember he once told me that 'the North East hadn't had an Olympic Gold medallist and I think you could be the one' so that was nice. Well that was more than nice because I thought 'well Brendan must know what he's talking about. Or was he just being nice?' No this is the North East, people aren't nice for the sake of being nice, what I mean is if they are nice, then they are genuinely nice. So to have Brendan Foster give me that opinion, to me I saw that as an endorsement of my potential, and that, as it would be for any athlete, was a terrific boost.

CJ: Did you really, really believe him?

JE: Mmmm . . . I don't know really, I think I did, but anyway, it didn't really change anything for me in the fact that all I could continue to do was work hard – and hope. Having Brendan say that was better than had he said nothing, or if he had said 'give up lad you haven't got a hope'. He knows how hard 'it' is and that my personal investment must show signs of bearing fruit to make it worthwhile, so I guess his words did, as I said give me a boost. It's odd isn't it, I wonder if he remembers those words? It's important you know that former athletes are responsible and say things that encourage – if they honestly believe that what they see in you really has potential. But ultimately it's about doing the hard work so that even if you never achieve anything spectacular in terms of championships, at least you can say to yourself – 'I tried my damn hardest' – and that is all anyone can do. So during that period I owed it to myself to keep pursuing my dreams, and that's what kept me going.

CJ: So tell me about the World Championships of 1995, in Gothenburg.

JE: Wow, Gothenburg, yes well I can remember the expectation leading up to it was immense. I had jumped well that year, in fact I had jumped 18.43m wind assisted at the European Cup, but I don't think I had quite anticipated ever being in that position, with the expectation that I would break the world record and become World Champion. It was overwhelming and I was completely scared stiff! I can remember Andy Norman organising a press conference – I think it was the one with you and Linford and you were both at that time world champions having won in Stutgartt in '93

CJ: Yep I remember it, although I wasn't competing in Gothenburg – injured, as ever!

JE: Well in the press conference, you two were in your element, and me, well I was just a bag of nerves what with all the attention I was getting. But Andy, in the middle of the press conference said that 'Jonathan Edwards will jump 18 metres'. Well he totally took me by surprise, and I looked at him and nearly said 'What?!?' So when you asked about heroes, for me, in the case of Brendan as well, it was a case of two people who at crucial stages of my career showed belief in my potential. That was the important thing for me.

CJ: Once you were in the stadium, did you feel there was a bit of magic in your legs?

JE: I knew from the form I was in, if I could get it right, I would jump a long way, I knew if I could respond to the environment in the stadium, then I could do well. I would need that adrenalin from the crowd if I was to jump far – because I could feed off that, I had learnt that lesson!

CJ: So you got through qualification, and in the first round of the final you are on the runway, and I can still remember the crowd's reaction to you.

JE: It was amazing for a field athlete to be the centre of attention, if you like. So often jumpers like me just got on with our stuff over on one side of the stadium while you guys got all the attention on the track – but I sensed this, for once, was different. And I was scared! There is no doubt whatsoever about that! I am telling you Colin what I had done was I bought a pair of sun glasses, without knowing what the weather was going to do – to hide my eyes as I didn't want to look in the eyes of any of my competitors in case they saw how scared I was! It was very intense, and the laughing and joking of the guys around the hotel suddenly goes, and there you are alone. Well alone with the crowd, a runway and a sand pit! My only thoughts were 'run fast and jump far!'

CJ: That's a really simple thought – and it worked.

JE: Well with that in my mind I took off down the runway, and when I landed my initial reaction was one of pure relief. Relief that I had nailed a jump, you never want to start with a foul or a run through the pit, you just want to post a distance and I could see it was somewhere around the 18m mark.

CJ: And when you saw the distance come up on the board . . . ?

JE: Well the crowd knew the actual distance before me, it came up on the board so they saw it and because there was a huge roar I am like surprised by it, and I look around thinking what . . . where, did someone throw a good javelin? It's my favourite moment of the TV coverage, and then I realise that I had done it, I had done it, I had actually, finally, broken the World Record.

CJ: But you didn't stop there?

JE: No I didn't stop there. That would not have been the case later on in my career because post 1995 once I led a competition I found it very difficult to find the level of adrenalin and motivation to do another long jump, unless someone else had jumped passed me. So I am not quite sure what it was that drove me – apart from a feeling that I knew I was ready to jump again, and jump long again. There was no lesser intensity of adrenalin going through my body, having broken the world record, and there is a big smile on my face before I take that second round jump as I thought to myself 'you may never get a moment like this again'. I knew going down the runway it would be further and that I would be breaking my own world record, and so when I landed in the pit I didn't need to look. I just knew it was even further.

CJ: What did it feel like?

JE: Well I picked myself up out of the sand and put out my hands to the crowd and shrugged my shoulders as if to say 'I don't know what happened there, but let me tell you, that is another world record actually! It just is!'

CJ: Those must have been amazing moments in time.

JE: So then I almost felt like I had a responsibility to the crowd to jump again. I was on a roll! I felt for the first time that people wanted to see me jump. So I obliged, almost knowing that it was going to be rubbish – and it was! So I should not have jumped, but hey! It was 17.50m which wasn't bad, but in the context of the previous two – it was complete rubbish! Isn't it great to be able to say that about a 17.50m jump! Rubbish! But that whole season had been great, I know you had periods in your career Colin when you knew if you performed you would win. I just put on my spikes and it was as easy as shelling peas. It's never been like that since.

CJ: It was a dream come true for you then.

JE: It was indeed a dream come true. It was the first 18m triple jump legal, first 60ft triple jump legal, and it still stands. All those times of disappointment, of self doubt, just disappeared and I was overwhelmed with the fact that I had found inside me what I always believed to have been there – and I had delivered it – and delivered it in a World Championship final. Undoubtedly that was my day. That was 'the day' of my athletics career.

CJ: I have got goose pimples again! Do you have any advice for young – or remembering your early years, not so young – sports men and women reading this?

JE: In the first instance if you are to get the best out of yourself you have got to love what you do. You have to want to do that thing for its own sake, and not for any other reason. Fundamentally that's what drove me to be as good as I was. I loved what I did. But also my story says – believe in yourself and never give in.

CJ: Do you still feel like an athlete?

JE: No! I definitely don't feel like an athlete now, it was just a separate existence! I never had much aerobic fitness as a triple jumper so although that has improved with all the cycling I do in the Lake District, no I am no longer an athlete. Don't make me laugh!

CJ: How do we get more youngsters into athletics?

JE: We have to inspire them. Saying that sport will get you healthy and give you discipline and focus and all that, that doesn't inspire kids. They are by-product benefits yes, but not the inspiring force. The London Olympics must play a huge role. The Olympics are still a magical occasion that captures all people's imaginations and I think it will capture young people's imaginations in a way that it wouldn't have done had it been in Paris or Moscow or New York. It is all about how you make the most of that opportunity, and we talk about legacy, and what is the legacy of hosting the Olympic Games in this country? I think the main one has to be inspiring young people. They have so many things vying for their attention and sport has to play by those rules and come up with exciting and innovative ways to inspire youngsters and entice them into sport – not in a way that tries to make them feel 'this is good for me', but because they will want to do it.

CJ: I hope you are right, I think the success of the London Olympics won't be measurable until years after the event. Let's hope it achieves that. Thanks J.

JE: Back to the house for a coffee?

CJ: I like the sound of that.

Jonathan Edwards CBE

Medals at major championships

Olympic Games

GOLD	2000	Sydney	Triple Jump
SILVER	1996	Atlanta	Triple Jump

World Championships

GOLD	1995	Gothenburg	Triple Jump
GOLD	2001	Edmonton	Triple Jump
SILVER	1997	Athens	Triple Jump
BRONZE	1993	Stuttgart	Triple Jump
BRONZE	1999	Seville	Triple Jump

European Championships

GOLD	1998	Budapest	Triple Jump
BRONZE	2002	Munich	Triple Jump

Commonwealth Games for England

GOLD	2002	Manchester	Triple Jump
SILVER	1990	Auckland	Triple Jump
SILVER	1994	Victoria	Triple Jump

Personal Best

Triple Jump – 18.29 [WR] 1995
18.43 m W +2.4 1995 (wind assisted)
100 m – 10.48 sec
Long jump – 7.41 m

b. 10th May 1966. London.

Jonathan is one of the very few athletes who have held the Grand Slam of titles at the same time namely the Olympic, World, Commonwealth and European titles. Indeed there were few titles he did not manage to win.

Jonathan attended West Buckland School where his potential for the triple jump was spotted at an early age, and on leaving received the school's top award for sporting and academic excellence, the Fortescue Medal.

Early success was won at the 1990 Commonwealth Games in Auckland with a bronze medal with a jump of 16.93m.

Due to his faith as a Christian he initially chose not to compete on a Sunday and missed the 1991 World Championships because of this. Despite the qualifying round being on a Sunday, he did choose to compete in the 1993 World's in Stuttgart and came home with a bronze medal

Jonathan's breakthrough year proved to be 1995 when he produced an astonishing jump of 18.43 m (60 feet 5½ inches) at the European Cup. His jump was wind assisted and therefore did not count as an official record. He remained unbeaten that year and went to Gothenburg for the World Championships where he broke the world record twice. On his first jump, he became the first man to pass the 18-metre barrier by jumping 18.16 m (59 feet 7 inches). The record lasted for about 15 minutes, as he then jumped a distance of 18.29m which made him the first man to jump 60 feet. As of today that record still stands.

The 1996 Atlanta Olympics didn't turn out as he would have liked! He was pre games favourite, but it was American Kenny Harrison who took it with a jump of 18.09m. Jonathan's silver medal jump of 17.88m was the longest ever jump not to have won gold!

His Olympic day came in 2000 at the Sydney Games where he won gold with a 17.71m jump and he returned to an adoring British public. His success was unprecedented after that and he took gold at the 2001 World Championships in Edmonton with a season's best of 17.92m. Commonwealth Games gold followed at Manchester in

2002. The World Championships in Paris in 2003 proved to be his final event, where Jonathan realised enough was enough. He retired without taking his full complement of qualifying jumps when it was evident that he was not on form. He refused to blame a niggling ankle injury, and asked his wife Alison who was sitting in the stand, whether it was ok for him to stop.

Jonathan has become a regular part of the BBC athletics commentary team.

Oscar Pistorius

"I love it. I love it, I love it, I love it."

Oscar is the Usain Bolt of the Paralympic world.

I've chosen Oscar for this book because he is one of South Africa's most exciting athletes, and I can honestly say every time I watch him perform, I always wonder if he's going to set a new world record! That is great for any crowd to anticipate and watch, and is a great benchmark for any sporting icon of mine! I marvel at his achievements. I forget he is a 'disabled' athlete – for me he is a great athlete. He goes through 'heartache' on a daily basis just to go out on the track to perform. There are so many things I take for granted that I can do. It takes Oscar twenty minutes to get ready for training when it takes me two minutes. So if quitting something ever crosses your mind step back from it for just a moment, and take a look at him. Oscar is inspirational in his own right.

He is so often caught up at the centre of arguments over whether he should be allowed to compete on a world stage against able bodied athletes, and the politics of that sometimes takes the focus away from his amazing performances on the track. His enthusiasm and love of his sport is evident and he does himself, and the sport of athletics proud.

Oscar is the headline act, and he carries that well. He just goes out there and does it. He is the self proclaimed 'fastest man on no legs' and I caught up with him at the track in Manchester as he practised in the starting blocks.

CJ: Do you know that many people who watch you, including me, do so expecting you to break records!

OP: I think it's a great complement, and I am glad if people think of me in that way. I set my first world record the day after I ran a 5K so I was quite stiff, so on each race day I am capable of running fast times, and yes I go out to try and do that.

CJ: How did you get into athletics then?

OP: Well when I was young I played a bit of soccer and tennis, and then started rugby and water polo in high school. In 2003 I broke my knee when I was playing rugby, it's such a hard game, and it was pretty bad. As part of my rehabilitation I started at the High Performance Centre in Pretoria and kind of got into athletics there. My coach Ampie Louw introduced me, and sort of pulled me into the whole athletics scene, and began entering me into competitions and before I knew it had just taken off. So before I could get back to rugby the following season, I was firmly stuck in athletics! I didn't know much about how to run the races and I didn't know much about the sport, and I can remember going to the US for a competition where I won well, and I was then shortlisted for the Athens Paralympic Games which was kind of mind blowing! It was a real roller coaster, and I admit I was really raw, you know I would just pitch up to meets and I would be running next to the World Champion or the World Record holder and I wouldn't even know who he was! In a way it must have worked for me because I didn't have any extra stress that way! I just sort of did the best I could, the only way I knew how!

CJ: So literally you were just raw talent!

OP: Well I guess so and I just got drawn into it. Fate played a hand I guess.

CJ: Any regrets?

OP: Wow no, none at all, it's been a wonderful journey so far and there is more to come.

CJ: What's the best bit about athletics?

OP: I guess the feeling that after months and months of hard training a competition goes well, and for yourself and the people around you, that is such a relief – so when in the race you realize it is going to turn out well, that is a great feeling.

CJ: For me being retired, I mean I've been on the shelf for quite some time, boy do I miss that feeling which I used to love. It's the feeling of winning. I would get that child like excitement like at Christmas time and it's almost an indescribable buzz . . .

OP: Yes for me it's a mixture between a fairy and a space cadet in anti gravity . . .

CJ: It's good to know those feelings don't change, but sometimes when the guys carrying the baskets left the start area and I was about two minutes away from the start of the race I did sometimes think why do I put myself through this pressure!

OP: Yes and knowing that 20 seconds after the start of the race you will know the outcome, that always spooks me. Then if you win about 1 second after you cross the line you just feel YES! I want to do that again! The best feeling for me is crossing the line first and then easing up after the line, when you are not racing but still travelling very, very fast, just bouncing along that's a great feeling. At the moment I can't imagine what it will be like after retiring and not having the chance to feel that! It always reminds me to appreciate it right here and now. In sport careers can be short, or at least the periods of your career when you are winning can be short, and of course can be cut short by injuries or whatever, so yes I do feel privileged that I am in the situation right now where that feeling is still mine to enjoy.

CJ: Yes it is pretty sweet, and that's what athletics does right!

OP: Yes, stress and relief, stress and relief. It's a rollercoaster ride and the peaks and troughs, the ups and downs, the highs and lows are what the sport is all about for an athlete. That's what the fans don't sometimes see, or maybe don't appreciate.

CJ: It's weird! You make me wish I was young again ready to step back on the track. Did you have any heroes when you were young?

OP: I have always been a boxing fan so Lennox Lewis was the coolest for me, but in other sports when I see someone being the best, I do admire that because you can almost say well he or she is the best because they do this, then this, then this. For anyone to be at the top of their sport – that demands respect. Seeing that success makes me feel like 'well if they can do that then there is no real reason why I can't do it as well', and it's been an inspiration for me to get where I am today.

CJ: So which event do you enjoy running the most?

OP: Well it's got to be the short sprints there's so much adrenalin involved, it's such a burst of energy and emotion. I love watching Asafa Powell and Usain Bolt run because they look so chilled you could almost think they weren't trying their hardest but I know that underneath their cool exterior, everything is flat out! Being able to control and maintain that calm chilled exterior is a real skill. To be able to put everything you have into it, and not have arms flailing around and your head rolling, that's what performing under pressure is.

CJ: Is it hard for you to keep everything under control? Talk me through a 200m race for you.

OP: Well the night before the race I always go to the track and imagine myself in the race, which is important for me, to visualise that. Then that evening I eat potatoes and spaghetti, and the next day from the time you go onto the track its nerve racking. So much time and effort will have been put into the preparation by me and the team around me, that the will to win is immense, and the knowledge that it will all be over in such a short space of time really focuses the . . . the pressure. When I get into the blocks then I really have to work hard, and concentrate on my starts. So for me its big arms and head down, and then really get my body position up, hips up and shoulders up, power on and control it. Coming off the bend of the 200 metres I cut to the inside of the lane and let rip! I just move down into third gear and catapult myself out of the last bit of the curve and into overdrive, and swing it home. The straight is the best bit of the race for me, try and maintain it all the way, try and enjoy it! Then the last ten metres just draw it all in, maintain overdrive, control it to the line, dip, lean, squeeze every last ounce of effort into that. The thickness of a vest can win it sometimes. Then as I mentioned, float and enjoy, float and enjoy the moment before your body slows and the party is over.

CJ: Is it at all painful for you?

OP: No not at all. Well it isn't if I have 'broken my blades in' and that can take a while.

CJ: So you are working on starts out of the blocks today then?

OP: Yes it's so crucial to me, to any sprinter I mean. You are perfect to give me some advice, you were pretty nifty out of the blocks as I remember.

CJ: I wasn't bad! It's the business part of the race, and I agree with what you said about the end, it can certainly come down to the thickness of a vest, so I always made sure I dipped for the tape.

OP: You dipped under the tape Colin, I read you were the photo finisher's nightmare cos you were out of the picture close to the ground most of the time!

CJ: Hahah, it certainly won me a few races I can tell you. But I've been watching you now and you look good out of the blocks.

OP: At the moment I am trying to break these new blades in, the old one's are falling apart and so I need to get used to these blades and to feel comfortable in them before I switch them to being my racing blades. Yes my block starts are improving. Practise makes perfect. I've run 21.58s for the 200m what's your best time Colin?

CJ: It's 21.19s and I never, ever lost a 200m race. But I only ever ran five! What do you think about when you get into the blocks?

OP: Good question. I think about getting out of the blocks! I think about the stages of exiting the blocks, and some say you shouldn't pay any attention to the runners around you – but I can hear them breathing! So I still find that I can't block that out!

CJ: Yes you can hear them breathing – and growling and grunting in some cases! You are bound to be aware of them, but don't let it be a distraction, try and accept its part of the start environment – then let it go. If those first few strides out of the blocks are good then they will give you the opportunity to win the race at the other end.

OP: Yes you can win the race right here, down this end of the track! It didn't distract you then, the shenanigans that go on in the blocks?

CJ: No never. There are a lot of photos of me in standing behind my blocks, focussed, staring down the track. I hardly recognise myself when I see them now. Commentators used to say it was a look of complete and utter concentration, an athlete in the zone. All I remember is a frightened feeling! In the hurdles you are on the edge of disaster for the whole race, because hitting a hurdle can end up in a catastrophic crash landing! But the start is an amazing skill to perfect. You do look pretty cool with it, and yes as always, practise does makes perfect.

OP: Do you know I always put my right blade on first. Why do I do that?

CJ: Are you superstitious?

OP: I don't think so! Well when I was at Athens my mates bought me a St Christopher necklace which I started wearing all the time. But then during one race I caught my finger in it and ripped it off accidentally. I did break the World 400m record for the first time in that race, but afterwards I thought I don't really want to get to believe in something and then one day drop it or lose it, and risk messing my mind up over it! So no I am not superstitious. It must be habit.

CJ: I've worked on the Paralympic Games it's a truly great sporting event.

OP: You know the Paralympics have taught me so much – it's something you will never, ever, ever, ever, ever find in any other competition. It's hard to comprehend, and very difficult to put into words how it is so special. The crowds at the Paralympics tend to be the biggest we race in front of and that is an experience as well. I love running under pressure at big championships where the passion of the crowd and the importance of the occasion demand more from you as an athlete. I love it when the long jumpers clap their hands above their head and encourage the crowd to do the same and they then try and feed off that – I would love to do that one day, in the blocks of the 100m maybe! Now that would be a first! But that's how I feel, I love to feel the crowd is with me, willing me on, and willing me to do well for their entertainment. I am sure it would make such a huge difference, I must try it.

CJ: I hope I am there to see it and enjoy it. What do you enjoy outside athletics?

OP: I enjoy golf and that gets a bit frustrating at times, but taking a long walk is the reward and if I don't play well, then I can gather my thoughts and go through stuff. That's awesome about it, and many a solution to certain problems has been found on a golf course. I like painting and reading, not at the same time, and I am a slow reader so I haven't got through many books! I bought a book the other day and read 80 pages in three days, so I am getting there. I do like motorbikes but I can't do much and risk injury, but the outdoors is for me.

CJ: What still motivates you in athletics?

OP: That's simple. I love athletics, I love it, love it, love it! It's so much fun; just talking about it gets me excited. The people around me in athletics, my mates and my coach motivate me, and in particular other athletes at the Paralympic events motivate me greatly. I know a US swimmer who has one arm and you see that guy swimming butterfly and you just got to sit back and think Wow! This is mind blowing stuff, and that motivates me, and seeing guys put so much effort into something they are so passionate about and when they get their rewards, they are inspiring. I was born with the fibula missing in both my legs and when I was one year old they amputated both my legs below the knee. So I guess my journey through athletics is unique or nearly unique. But I feel like any other athlete in that, of course, winning races motivates me.

CJ: Well I hope you continue to enthral crowds wherever you race, and keep being such a great ambassador for the sport of athletics, because you love athletics and people sense that when they meet you and when they see you on the track – and that is great for the sport.

OP: Oh that's real kind to say that Colin, I really appreciate that. I really do. See you in Cape Town or Johannesburg sometime.

Oscar Pistorius

Medals at major championships

Paralympics

GOLD	2004	Athens	T44 200m
GOLD	2008	Beijing	T44 100m
GOLD	2008	Beijing	T44 200m
GOLD	2008	Beijing	T44 400m
BRONZE	2004	Athens	T44 100m

IPC World Championships

GOLD	2006	Assen	T44 100m
GOLD	2006	Assen	T44 200m
GOLD	2006	Assen	T44 400m
GOLD	2010	Manchester	T44 100m
GOLD	2010	Manchester	T44 400m

Paralympic World Cup

GOLD	2005	Manchester	T44 100m
GOLD	2005	Manchester	T44 200m
GOLD	2006	Manchester	T44 100m
GOLD	2006	Manchester	T44 200m
GOLD	2007	Manchester	T44 100m
GOLD	2007	Manchester	T44 200m
GOLD	2009	Manchester	T44 100m
GOLD	2009	Manchester	T44 400m

b. 22nd November 1986. Sandton, Johannesburg.

Oscar is the world record holder in his category for the 100m, 200m and 400m sprints. At the Beijing Paralympic Games in 2008 he became the first athlete to win gold in all three sprint events.

Born without the fibula in both legs, Oscar was only 11 months old when his parents, Henke and, sadly the late Sheila, made the heart-wrenching decision to have his limbs amputated below the knee. At Pretoria Boy's High School he excelled in rugby, water polo and tennis, but in January 2004 he shattered his right knee playing rugby.

At the age of 17, he ran the 100m in an open competition at the Pilditch stadium in his hometown of Pretoria after training for only two months. He ran it in 11.51s; the world record was 12.20s.

Eight months later he lined up in the Athens Paralympic Games, proudly representing South Africa, and he proved to be a sensation taking bronze behind Americans Marlon Shirley and Brian Frasure in the 100m. Marlon Shirley was the defending double Paralympic champion at the 100m and 200m and yet Oscar went on to win gold in the 200m and break the world record in 21.97s.

At the South African Championships in March 2005, Oscar finished in 6th place in the 400m open/able-bodied category, and in the same year, he won the gold in both the 100m and 200m at the Paralympic World Cup in Manchester.

He took the 400m silver medal in the 2007 South African National Championships competing against able-bodied runners.

The 2008 Paralympic Games in Beijing were a triumph for Oscar as he shaved a further 0.3 seconds off his 200m record bringing it to 21.67s. He also won the 100m in a record time of 11.16s, and also took gold in the 400m in a world record time of 47.49s. Oscar secured himself a place in the history books by becoming the first ever Paralympian to win gold in all three events.

In 2010 Oscar set a new record of 47.04s in winning the 400m race at the Diamond League meeting in London's Crystal Palace. At the same meet he ran in an able bodied race and clocked 46.93s which was not eligible for record status as the event was not sanctioned by the International Paralympic Committee.

In 2006, Oscar was conferred the Order of Ikhamanga in Bronze (OIB) by the President of South Africa as acknowledgement for his outstanding achievements in sport.

In 2007 Oscar was awarded the BBC Sports Personality of the Year Helen Rollason Award, which is given for outstanding courage and achievement in the face of adversity.

www.oscarpistorius.co.za

Tessa Sanderson

"As a young girl I would run and hide – but now there was nowhere left to run to."

I arranged to meet Tessa at her office in Newham, London, and she had assembled all the staff for a group photo and had me signing autographs for the children. She cared about them that was obvious, but that's Tessa in a nutshell. When I was just starting out on my career she took me under her wing and took care of me. She was the comfort breast for many on the team. She was like a mother figure, although she would smack me for saying that! She was so successful yet she still had the time of day for you and was . . . just like your mother, or a big sister. If you had problems the first person you would run to was Tessa and she always seemed to have something wise to say. I had huge respect for her because she achieved so much against the odds.

Tessa used to come down to stay in Cardiff many a time and all my family loved her. She was a big star and yet so down to earth.

She looked good today, very well groomed, and her energy and enthusiasm for her role with the Newham Academy of Sport was plain to see. Her rivalry with Fatima Whitbread is legendary, but behind that hard competitive exterior Tessa can be quite apprehensive about her own ability – which is not always a bad thing as an athlete. As we sat down she showed me a book someone had brought in for her.

CJ: Wow, it's the Olympic Games London 1948 handbook and look, here it says 'The catering centre will have a self service system enforced and all Chef de Missions are reminded that owing to rationing visitors cannot, on any pretext, be entertained in the team's dining room.'

TS: Due to rationing wow! Oh it's a wonderful handbook, and there is a bit where it asks that certain competitors bring their own sandwiches! Fantastic!

CJ: Well Tessa what's happening here then?

TS: Its almost like my second home it really is, we are at the Newham Borough 2012 office, and a lot of the strategic side for the 2012 Olympics is coming out of here. My main role here has been to establish the Newham Sport Academy, and there is a lot of talent around here that can be nurtured but they never get the opportunity. So I hope my 26 years of track and field experience can help us engage with the best coaches in the country, across a lot of the Olympic sports, to help bring some talent up to the next level. It's important to start to do this in Newham as it's the host borough for 2012.

CJ: It wasn't like this in your or my day, things were different – you weren't born in the UK were you? Tell me a little about your younger days.

TS: No I came to Britain when I was six. It was such a shell shock, honestly! I was born in Jamaica, and I lived with my grandmother Robertha, or Miss Spongey we called her, and you know what it's like, in the Caribbean although I lived with my grandmother she was like my mother really. I remember when my Mum and Dad sent a letter over saying they were ready for me and my older sister to come over to join them here in Britain, I ran away and went and hid in the hills. I was so happy with my grandmother and so well looked after and loved by her, and I was so afraid of the stories that it was so cold in Britain that if you touched your nose it would fall off! Honestly these were the things that were said at that time!!

Well they eventually found me hiding, and that was that, we were soon on our way from Jamaica to Britain.

CJ: What was that like for a six year old?

TS: Well I can remember flying; I was flying Colin at six years old! I remember we flew on a BOAC flight into Manchester and the first thing I remember is standing on the aeroplane steps and seeing all this smoke coming out of my mouth as my warm breath hit the cold air because it was bloody freezing! All I could think was what's all this then?! And there I stood holding my sister's hand waiting for my parents to meet us. It was an absolute shell shock for us, it was freezing, it was foggy, it was dark, it was bleak and I thought why the hell have I come here for! I didn't really know what to expect because my Mum left for Britain when I was one, along with my Dad, you know they were what are now known as 'the boat people' who came here to get work. But they had never forgotten us in Jamaica and they worked hard towards getting us over.

CJ: Where did you go first from Manchester then?

TS: Well we went to live in Wolverhampton, in the West Midlands, and I spent most of my school days there, and that's where I grew up really until I got into track and field which took me away travelling. The people were great and I remember another shell shock though, I had never seen snow in my life, and everyone was rolling about in it and I thought they must be off their heads! The people were really wonderful, but it took me a long time to come to terms with the dialect and West Midland accent. The one thing I found I hated was chips! In Jamaica we call these Irish potatoes or something like that, and the first time I tasted them uhhh! There were very few spices used in the English food so I missed the Jamaican food terribly and the recipes that my grandmother used to make. But the funny thing is that's what started me off in athletics.

CJ: Chips?

TS: Yes chips! Well a bet for a bag of chips! When I was in school my friend called Noreen Morgan, a tall skinny girl she was, and although I was doing well in sport at jumping and running, I could not beat her at the javelin. So what happened was she made a bet with me, she said in her thick Wolves accent 'Yeow Teraysa, cyn yaw beat me at javelin?' so I said 'Wew Yeow aw wight I will take you on girl!' So come school sports day I was all prepared and I had practised a bit before hand – sorry Noreen you never knew I trained for that day – but I did!! I was getting it together, and I never forget the feeling as that javelin went whoosh, it went so far, and I won, and the bet had been that the loser would buy the chips for the whole week. Now chips were about tuppence a bag and I had really grown to love them with all that salt and vinegar, and Colin that week it was like being in heaven – I could save all my money to spend in the sweet shop and spent all Noreen's in the chip shop. Now that's the way to do it!

CJ: So the start of Tessa Sanderson's athletics career started in the chip shop!

TS: Yes it did, it absolutely amazing to think that is how I started, because I really got the bug for the javelin. So thanks again Noreen Morgan!! Love you.

CJ: How did your parents react to you picking up athletics?

TS: Well I guess I may have been a little spoilt by my dear Dad, he called me his little darling, and if I didn't really fancy going training on a wet or windy night – then he didn't force me. At the start they were not really very keen on me giving up so much time to athletics. When I started in 1969 I think it was terribly difficult as in the late 1960s and early 70s there was a lot of racism around, and your parents tried to protect you as best they could. I mean there were incidents, you know Colin, the usual stuff.

CJ: But you were very young so you probably can remember, because you don't forget that sort of thing!

TS: Well you know what kids can be like – so cruel!! So most of it was that type of thing, but there were a few incidents that I can never forget, I do remember being spat at in school, and being called a golliwog, and a nigger. You know it was the 1960s and immigration was new to everyone, so it was at its very worse then.

CJ: Little did they guess you were to become the first British black woman to win an Olympic Gold medal! Do you know Tessa what really used to get my back up during my career? One minute a guy would be walking down the street calling me a nigger – and the next minute he would be cheering me as I won a race. That I find disgusting and impossible to deal with.

TS: Yes but anyhow my Mum and Dad wanted me to be a nurse! But I knew the first time I saw blood – phew that's not for me ta! But they did want me to try and get a career behind me, which I can understand now, that's probably the same for every parent to wish that for their kids. My parents looked at it and thought I would need a career to fall back on if the athletics didn't work out, I mean through injury or whatever, and as it happened late in my career I did get injured and felt lucky I had my secretarial skills to fall back on. Anyway no, when I started competing my parents didn't want me to become a track and field athlete, but I had a superb teacher called Barbara Richards, and she came to my house and talked to my parents.

CJ: There is always someone isn't there, we all have them, they make the difference. Unsung heroes!

TS: Now my Mum and Dad couldn't always afford to get me to the stadiums, or pay for travel here and there. At that time my Dad was a steelworker and he worked shifts so he would often be home sleeping during the day. My Mum would often sneak into the bedroom to get 20p out of his trouser pocket to pay for the bus to the training track, and me and my sister would be giggling by the door. Some years later I found out that he wasn't always sleeping just pretending and he knew we were taking it – and he knew why I needed it. So that was all very funny in the end, but the truth was we couldn't really afford it, so Barbara helped out there as well, and she helped show my Mum and Dad that this was for real, it was something I really enjoyed, and that I wasn't neglecting my studies. After that chat, they were 100% behind me.

I mean I've always said that I have been very lucky to have been born to the parents I had, because they mean the world to me, Mum is like another sister to me, and my sister and I have never had a fight in fifty odd years, we have never had a major row, I have two wonderful brothers as well and my Dad is one in a million – we are such a close family, I am very lucky. They have been so supportive to me and I now have a tear coming so I will stop there!

CJ: Here take this hanky. I couldn't wait to talk to my parents after a race, it was important, win or lose, they always knew what I would be going through!

TS: Oh dear, thanks Colin, yes exactly, my Dad is such an amazing guy, and what happened in the 1984 Olympic Games the night before my competition I rang home to say I am feeling OK, all is well, and to see how things were back home. From what I could gather over the phone all the family and loads of friends had brought their sleeping bags round my parent's house and they were going to sleep over and watch me competing on the telly. Well apparently my Dad had enough and said 'I am off to bed – wake me when my little darling has won.'

The next morning when he woke up and found out that I had indeed won, he opened the front door and shouted all the way down the street! I rang home afterwards desperate to speak with them all and Dad came on the phone and said 'Helo my golden girl' and that got me in here, in my heart, and I shed a few tears I can tell you. That stuck with me ever since, because you are not just competing for yourself, you are competing for your family and close friends, your coaches, and those moments that I shared with my family I just won't forget those.

CJ: Did you have a sporting hero?

TS: Yes! In 1977 I started work with the Variety Club of Great Britain, and I was told that there was to be a function at the Sportsmen's Club in the West End – with Mohammed Ali. Yes! Mohammed Ali the icon, the God on this planet in sport and I thought I must meet him, he must meet me! So I was asked along, and asked to bring something to present to him, so I brought him a photo of me. Yes, I am as vain as you Colin!

CJ: No way, impossible! Impossible! So you had the audacity to present him with a picture of you! You getting close to me girl!

TS: I know how dare I! But you know what, I never wanted him to forget me. The picture was massive, I had it enlarged specially! Too right Colin, no way was he going to forget me, I could just about carry it! I was so nervous and just before I met him I had huge second thoughts, and doubted whether I should give it to him. In the end I thought oh stuff it – and I did give it to him, I did. He must have slung it straight in his attic!

CJ: No way! It's probably hanging in his bedroom, hanging above his bed!

TS: Hahaha. It was a great moment for me to meet him, he was just fantastic. Colin you know what, I think I love him a little bit more than I love you my darling.

CJ: Well I better leave I think. Now when you win something amazing, like an Olympic Gold and you become the golden girl of British athletics, how did you deal with that?

TS: Hee hee was I the golden girl? You didn't tell me. No, for me it was a little bit different, because up to the Olympics in 1984 there was so much rivalry going on between me and my mate Fatima Whitbread. I felt though that it wasn't just Fatima that I had to fight. I had to fight British Athletics and the British Amateur Athletics Board, and I felt that no-one was doing anything to help me – and they weren't. I was getting really frustrated because a lot of my competitions were getting taken off, and I couldn't get enough competitions and the build up was all for Fatima, and she was getting the profile and she was getting the sponsorship deals – and I just felt that since there were two good javelin throwers in the UK that we both should be supported.

CJ: You and Fatima really were head to head all the time!

TS: Yes the rivalry was so intense and the media hyped it for all it was worth. I think we did hate each other at one stage because I wanted to win and Fats wanted to win, and we both tried to channel that intense rivalry to try and gain a few more centimetres! But we are older and wiser now, and the handbags have been put away. But back then, my goodness it was fierce.

CJ: So going into the Olympics in 1984, Los Angeles that rivalry was at a peak really!

TS: Yes it was, and it was very frustrating for me – ok admittedly Fatima was throwing very well, but Tina Lilak of Finland was the World Record holder and we both needed to be helped to go out there and beat up on her and the rest of the world! So I went there feeling quite frustrated at all this, and felt that apart from my family and a few supporters there was no-one really there behind me. However, low and behold I was wrong – to a certain extent because once I had got to the Olympics and the competition time was approaching, one person I was grateful for being there for me, was Mary Peters. She was just fantastic. I had admired her as an athlete in the days when we were competing and I wanted to try and emulate a lot of what she had done, and at the 1984 Olympics she was our team manager and she gave me a lot of . . . confidence.

I remember the morning of the competition there was a knock at my door and it was Mary telling me to get up and have breakfast. I remember my heart was pounding so fast, but a few words from Mary settled me.

CJ: What were you thinking at the Stadium then, because lacking confidence going into an Olympic final sounds worrying.

TS: Well there was a little incident that put me at ease. I was in the warm up area and I always take a little ball which I throw against the wall to loosen up my shoulder as the start of my warm up, but there were no walls. It was just a vast expanse of a place with a tree in the middle. So I start throwing the ball against the tree, and my shoulder is starting to loosen when the ball gets stuck up this blooming tree, high up in the branches! Well I can't leave it there, so I have to get my javelin and try and try and try and reach the damn thing. So there I am halfway up a tree with a javelin trying to get this ball down, not long before going into the Olympic stadium. I wanted my ball!! So by the time I fished it down it was time to go to the call room and I was feeling rather relaxed and good!

CJ: It settled your mind, took your mind off it, cos it's a tense time.

TS: Yes, and there is so much psychology involved in these things its mad really. When I arrived in the call room I notice that Fatima is sitting there next to Tina Lilak, and a small gap in the middle between them. Well it was like King Kong next to Godzilla and if I was going to die it would be there and then. So I thought where do I sit? For a second I almost went to a free space further over, and then thought, no this is a test of character. So in I went and planted myself right there in between the two of them, and started coolly to put on my boots. Soon enough the call came for us to go out to the infield, and that moment is so hard Colin it can be so difficult, and out we went and the crowd was shouting our names, and Sharon Gibson another British thrower was there as well. And we began the first round and it was very hard to comprehend because I felt scared, I felt nervous, I wanted to be sick, and like that little girl back home in Jamaica, all those years ago, I wanted to run off and hide – but there was nowhere left to run to!

CJ: So what had changed you, what enabled you to . . . to stand your ground?

TS: My coach Wilf Parish had instilled in me, if you like, the understanding of being a gladiator . . . he used to say that you could do all the preparation, all the training, get into shape, get the technique right – but when the time came to step out into that arena then it was your own private war. It was going to be tough and mentally it could be bloody nasty, but it was my battle and only I could fight it.

CJ: So game on then!

TS: Yes. I thought this is it. This is the time to go. Fatima went in and threw and released her almighty roar – aaaahhhhhhhhhh!!!! She does roar very loud. Then Tina Lilak was also throwing before me, and if there was a time that I wanted to be throwing after them two it was then! Tina came down the runway and released the javelin – she too roared – eeehhhhhhh!! But her roar was a higher pitch and not quite as loud as Fats. I remember watching her thinking how tall and blond and elegant she was and how I imagined her shouting after the javelin 'Get out there darling javelin, fly yonder dear javelin, fly like a bird.' They were both pretty good throws

CJ: Now Tina at this time was World Champion?

TS: Yes she was, and having watched her, I suddenly thought 'Oh my God it's my turn'. So I got on the runway and settled myself, and said to myself 'Yeaow Teraysa, this is it! This reaaally is it.' And I forgot all the injuries of the previous two years, everything just went out of my head, and all I wanted to do was to throw my whole body and my whole self into that javelin and let it go out, and as long as I did myself justice it would be ok. I stood there holding the javelin up, with the fingers of my other hand twitching. I was telling myself leg down quick, leg down quick, right body into it, shoulders back – the things I had repeated a million times before, and just before I started running down that runway, the last thing that went through my mind was 'Please God, let it be right!' I opened my eyes and off I went and gathered speed and then Bang! Launched that javelin, and I think I gave the biggest shout of us all, it was a seriously big shout – aaaahhhheeeehhhh!!!! And my body position and my bow felt absolutely perfect and my shoulders and my chest and everything went out after that javelin, and I stood there and watched it as it hit the turf and I said let it be right, let it be right. Well it must have been about two minutes before it came up 69m 56cm, a new Olympic Record. Ahhhhhhhhhh! I roared again Colin!! I roared!

CJ: To throw that in the first round though, that gave you a lot of scenarios to think about, and a lot of time to think as well.

TS: It did. Tina, Fats and me had all thrown longer leading up to the Games, so any one of us could reach that distance. So it was game on. Then it was like I locked my mind into this area, and I daren't look outside it, not at my competitors, not at the crowd. You just want to make sure that every single throw after that is right, because after the euphoria of setting a new Olympic record I thought where the heck do I go from that! Well we got to the final round, and Fatima did her best but had to settle for a bronze, and I was happy for her too. I was still leading and I would have been less happy if she were beating me. I can remember waiting for Tina to throw and I almost could not look.

CJ: Nerve racking stuff!

TS: I am telling you! She stood on the runway and I almost stood there with her! Almost asking her not to do it, not to throw it, not to spoil it for me! So up she came and the roar was almighty, oh what a roar, and I stood there looking, thinking this javelin is not coming down, its so big its not coming down, and I thought no, please don't let this happen, it can't happen.

Well it finally came down, and landed on 69m, and the rest is history. Dearest God, I got down on my knees and went like that, my arms in the air, and it was just fantastic. You know? It was just a moment of . . . everything. It was a feeling of complete euphoria and all that, but I still had one more throw and I didn't know whether to take it, but I did decide to take it.

It was on that throw I realised that I could feel the breeze once again on my face, the noise of the crowd registered again. Life itself came back to me. And standing on the runway for the last time I thought; guess what, I've whooped them all, I've gone and whopped them all this time! I am the new Olympic

Champion, and once I let that final throw go, I don't think I even waited for it come down,

I was away around the track celebrating like a mad woman – and field athletes didn't usually do that sort of thing, but I thought hey this is my time – and it was funny because at the other end of the stadium Carl Lewis was ready to take his jump and some American officials said to me 'hey lady, stop and get off the track m'am.' So I told them – 'no way, he didn't stop for my event, I ain't stopping for his' and away I went whoosh on around the stadium, it was amazing, amazing feeling! That was my moment. That was really 'my moment.'

CJ: And you rang home?

TS: Yes well by the time I had managed to produce a wee sample for the doping test straight afterwards, and got back to the accommodation block, everyone had left to go out. I rang home and that was a tearful call, loads of noise going on back there, with people crying and shouting well done, and me in tears. The relief was amazing, and all my family had shared in that achievement, it really was magical. I remember Daley Thompson calling round my room the next morning, and he was so lush, and handsome Colin, and he was just lovely and Daley gave me the biggest hug in the world.

CJ: So your day out at Buckingham Palace capped it all off right?

TS: Yes it did. I think the Queen is pretty damn special, and I don't care what any anti-royalists say, I really do love her, and I loved Diana when I worked with her on cerebral palsy charity and Princess Anne too. So yes I am very much pro Royal, and going over to the Palace is a wonderful treat and a wonderful honour, and when I did go to receive the CBE in 2002, for my efforts in sport and for the bits here and there I had been doing for special causes, it was such a special day not only for me – but for my whole family. It was their day out as well as mine.

CJ: From Jamaica to Wolverhampton to Buckingham Palace, that is some story, thanks Tessa.

TS: Give me a kiss honey.

Tessa Sanderson CBE

Medals at major championships

Olympic Games

GOLD	1984	Los Angeles	Javelin

European Championships

SILVER	1978	Prague	Javelin

Commonwealth Games for England

GOLD	1978	Edmonton	Javelin
GOLD	1986	Edinburgh	Javelin
GOLD	1990	Auckland	Javelin

Personal best

Javelin	73.58m

b. March 14, 1956 St. Elizabeth, Jamaica.

Tessa proved her longevity if nothing else by competing in a total of six Olympic Games, and for a woman who, after retiring, entered into a TV career on Sky Television, it was poetic that her Olympic victory should come in Hollywood, Los Angeles in 1984.

Tessa had been the dominant force in women's javelin for a decade before Fatima Whitbread came on the scene as a serious challenger to her dominance. That marked the start of a bitter rivalry between the two, which continued throughout their careers until Fatima had to quit in 1990 due to injury. It was by no means a two way competition for they had fierce rivals in Tina Lilak of Finland and Petra Felke of then East Germany, and it was this that rankled Tessa who believed British Athletics, and the British press would be better off supporting both Fatima and herself, rather than constantly playing one off against the other.

Her Olympic title, and her proudest moment came in 1984, with a throw of 69.56m, and she was the first British athlete ever to win a throwing event at the Olympics. Injuries unfortunately kept her out of the World Championships in Tokyo in 1991 – a year when she threw 65.18m at the European Cup and was confident of success that year. At the 1992 Barcelona Olympics she briefly led the competition with a throw of 63.58m but eventually missed out on a medal finishing in fourth place.

After four years of retirement Tessa returned to competition in 1996 and established a number of over-40 world bests during the season. She proudly took her place on the British team for the Atlanta Olympics in 1996 for an incredible sixth time, equalling the record of Romanian discus thrower Lia Manoliu. It was a fairytale ending to an illustrious career. Tessa won a total of 10 WAAA titles, her last coming in 1996. Of her first coach, she says John Morgan first spotted that she could run, jump and throw, and from there I just had this incredible competitive spirit from my family.

Tessa presented sports news for SKY TV after her retirement, before her return to athletics in 1996, and she also was vice chair of Sport England from 1999 to 2005. Her current work with London 2012 and the Newham Sports Academy allows her the opportunity to continue with a lifelong involvement and passion of helping and supporting children.

Her sporting achievements and her work with various charities and organisations were rewarded by the Queen in her honours list of which Tessa is particularly proud. Tessa recently married partner Densign White in St. Pauls Cathedral.

www.tsfa.co.uk

Sally Gunnell

"How much does it hurt? Oh – it's only the amount you do, and each individual training session that hurts."

I thought I would take Sally a present, and I decided on cream cakes. After seemingly spending an athletics lifetime together having to watch what we ate, I thought we could pig out together.

Sally is a Chigwell girl, an Essex girl, and we really grew up together since we set out on our careers at the same time, and we have had some laughs along the way! It was unreal really being able to share with my buddy the highs of athletics as we both made history in our sport. We started together as 17 year olds, and in 1992 we were voted by the IAAF as male and female athletes of the year and that really topped it all.

She lives in rolling countryside near the South Downs, in a 13th century farm house, with a tarmac drive long enough to allow me change up to second gear!

Not surprisingly she is still in great demand as a motivational speaker because her career journey, like many of my icons, held many twists and turns for her to negotiate on her way to success.

CJ: I come bearing gifts my darling!

SG: Hi, what have you got? Oh cream cakes, ok you can come and chat anytime!

CJ: Sally we go back a long way and I can remember your address when we were young and it was a farm near London right?

SG: Yes it was, I was brought up on a farm, and that love of open spaces is still with me. I grew up seeing my Dad work hard on the farm, seeing that mentality of being up really early in the morning and often working late especially at harvest time, so I definitely think that came into account when I left home, and had to work hard for myself. Later on a lot of the people I trained with were from the City of London and if we were training on Waltham Forest Track say, which is in a real city area of London, and I would say I am going home to the farm, because our farm was the closest farm to London, they would say 'how do you work that out!' But as you well know Colin I also liked getting out of the country and hitting the city lights!

CJ: Yes we did a bit of that in our time girl! Now how did you get into the sport at a young age then?

SG: I guess I just found something I was good at, I wasn't particularly academic, I wasn't musical or creative. But I had this natural ability to run fast, and I used to run up the field to see my Dad who would be on the combine harvester and run back again, and there were a lot of open spaces for me to run! I was in fact very good at gymnastics so I spent the ages of ten, eleven and twelve doing back flips and arrow springs around the house, and forever getting told off for doing cartwheels in the kitchen. I did smash through a window one day attempting a head stand. So at twelve years old my Mum and Dad said 'do you want to join a gymnastic club or do you want to join an athletic club because you are good at both.' I so nearly went to do gymnastics because I had been watching Nadia Comaneci and Olga Korbut and they were my real role models at that stage in life, and the sport seemed really glamorous. It was only because a friend of mine was going down to the athletic club that I decided well I might as well go with someone I know. So I joined the club at twelve years old and at fourteen was spotted by my coach Bruce Longden and by then I was hooked!

CJ: So what were your early experiences in The Essex Ladies Athletic club?

SG: Well our weekends away on club trips were my social life, and that's why I stayed in the sport really because I enjoyed the social side the club gave me, and these days that would be even more important because there are a lot more different clubs and societies all competing for children's attention. Some say if the kids don't want to do it then you can't make them – well I disagree. I think the clubs should take the responsibility to chase the kids, and all parents should be a positive influence and recognise that sport will be good for the children, and encourage them to attend. Athletics is fantastic, there is an event for everyone, it shouldn't cost a lot to do, and it's a great social scene to get into.

CJ: Were hurdles always the event for you?

SG: No not at all, I used to be called grasshopper because I had this natural spring and I started off as a long jumper and did that for many, many years and then Bruce Longden who had coached Daley Thompson in the decathlon had me doing multi events for some time, which gave me a real strength back ground. I do remember though, I went to some events and I was absolutely rubbish in things like shot put and javelin! And I could never high jump. I missed out from qualifying for the 1984 Olympics at the heptathlon and it was then that I decided to concentrate on the hurdles – the 100 metre hurdles! I was told by someone pretty high up in the British Athletics food chain that I was totally the wrong shape and the wrong colour to succeed at hurdle sprinting! I guess they didn't know, or at least underestimated, the determination I had in my heart and in my mind. Luckily I didn't listen – well no that's not quite the truth, I did hear the criticism, but I didn't let it deter my determination to do my best. Just goes to show

Colin, the only one to put a ceiling on what you might achieve – is yourself. Don't ever listen to anyone who puts you down – when they don't know YOU.

CJ: I remember being at the 1984 Commonwealth Games in Edinburgh and whilst I won silver for Wales in the 110 metre hurdles I remember seeing you win gold in the 100 metre hurdles and thinking how has she done that we are the same age!

SG: Yes I know and I think that was the first time that I believed in myself! I was two stone too heavy, I don't know how I got over the hurdles, and I lined up in the final next to my role model at that time Shirley Strong the British number one. Now Shirley used to smoke 30 a day – that's not why she was my role model – but I remember thinking oh wow she is going to win. I can't beat Shirley Strong! Then I thought, do I let her win or do I try and do my best and see if I can beat her? Well when I did win that was the first time I thought that I might be able to go and be world class. Then coach Longden told me I didn't have enough basic speed to make it at the 100 metre hurdles, and if I wanted to be the best in the world I should move up to the 400 metre hurdles.

CJ: And did you listen to him, did you respect that?

SG: Colin all I thought was that is going to hurt big time! Of course I respected that. Bruce knew me. So we spent the next two years doing both events but ultimately he was right, and I started to break British records at the first couple of 400mH races that I ran.

CJ: How painful was it?

SG: How much did it hurt? It's only the amount of sessions you do, and each individual training session that hurts.

CJ: Hahahaha – Is that all. That's ok then!

SG: Yes really, it was the long track sessions and being sick after – or during – them, and it took me a few years just to adapt to that sort of training. 'Why am I doing this' did cross my mind many, many, many times, but that early success kept me going. Learning stride patterns and learning the technical side was difficult but my multi event back ground and maybe my gymnastics helped with strength and learning the technical side. It took years to get it right – and did I ever get it right!! Well on one or two days I did get it right. Tell me Colin, your career wasn't exactly injury free?

CJ: Yes I had my fair share of niggles, knees mostly, cartilage, and I think the final tally was seven knee operations. But, as for a lot of us, because you are so focussed, you are tempted not to stop when you are carrying an injury, and that makes it worse in the end because you have to get it fixed at some stage and you then find that the wear and tear you have created by keeping on working your tired and injured muscles and joints then causes bigger problems. I had Gerard Hartman, over in Limerick to take care of me, I was there for ages at a time, and he is top notch. If it wasn't for him . . . well . . . I owe him!

SG: So what about after retiring – because for me that hurt when I didn't think it would!

CJ: Oh tell me about it! As my muscle tone started to fall away I began to have trouble with my back and my knees, and I found it was uncomfortable to sit still for any length of time.

SG: Yes I sometimes creak in the mornings!

CJ: So, you got fifth place in the Seoul Olympics in 1988, which announced that you had arrived as a quality hurdler, but can I ask you about the World Championships in 1991, in Tokyo, which weren't the best Championships for Britain really, and I remember you not being particularly happy but you came home with a silver medal.

SG: Well I can remember coming over the eighth hurdle with two to go and being in the lead and thinking I can win this. But I don't know what happened, maybe I started looking around but something happened I don't know, I lost concentration, ended up stuttering into the ninth hurdle and had a bit of a ding dong with Sandra Farmer-Patrick of the US, over that ninth hurdle. Well Tatyana Ledovskaya of the Soviet Union won and I remember coming away thinking 'I've just thrown away a gold medal, I've really mucked up, and I might not ever get that chance ever again', and that certainly made me more aware about what goes on in the mind. I hadn't focussed on what I was doing and I learnt a very hard lesson that day, which I wasn't ever going to allow myself to forget.

CJ: So did you take that through to the Olympics the following year 1992?

SG: I did and I had twelve months to get it right as Barcelona in 1992 was going to be my best chance for an Olympic Gold. I did a lot of work with the mind and learning to believe in myself. I was sorting that stride pattern out, because that stride pattern was more in the mind that anything else. I didn't really go into those games as the favourite which changes the way you think about things so that helped, and when I did win everyone expects the world of you then. But being an Olympic Champion didn't make the training any easier!

CJ: Great cherries my darling.

SG: Glad you like them Colin, yes they have come on beautifully this year. I love having so much space and I do a lot of thinking here in the garden. I have found a little corner which no-one else bothers with much, and I kind of call it my place where I can get a moment or two of peace and quiet.

CJ: Yes it's a real English country garden, I see a lot of wild flowers in here.

SG: Yes and the smell is lovely, and the bees and birds, it's very pleasant. Reminds me of my childhood having the countryside around me, I couldn't be anywhere else!

CJ: And I can see a beautiful English rose . . . .

SG: Yes it's finally come well this year, it was a bit slow in showing itself, but with a bit of care and attention it really has bloomed recently.

CJ: So to 1993 which is the race I am interested in!

SG: Yes I thought you might be! The World Championships in Stuttgart, where you also delivered and won Gold and set a new World Record Colin. Two mates together!

CJ: You were hot favourite, and expectations were upon you, it was a must win race, so what attitude did you take in there?

SG: It was a weird year really; I panicked half way through winter training that I hadn't done enough, but came out at the beginning of the year and found I was really in fantastic shape and thought wow this is amazing! I was running faster times than I had done at the Olympics, and I started to think about breaking that World record, and wondering could it be in there. So that was my state of mind leading up to Stuttgart, and then a week before the Championships I came down with flu cold. I felt absolutely awful and I could not believe it. I could not get out of bed and all I thought was there is no way I am going to be able to get around that track.

What I was scared of doing was pulling out and everyone saying well she can't cope with the pressure, because the expectation was massive. So I did not know what to do. I am one of those people who always ticks the box of standing on the line feeling 100%. So I decided to run the heats and semis to see what would happen and got through them, and did a great job acting like I wasn't ill, not letting any of my competitors know how dreadful I felt! And for the last 48 hrs before the final just spent using my mind to say 'you can do it, you can do it' while there was this little voice saying 'you can't, you can't you are ill, you're not well, you should be in bed!'

So I really stood on that line not sure what on earth was going to happen, and I must admit I don't really remember much of what happened in that race. Coming off the last hurdle I didn't realise I was behind Sandra Farmer-Patrick, I didn't really know I was chasing her down. I was in a little world of my own. I was running to plan and just hit hard off the last hurdle, and when I crossed the line I didn't know whether I was first, second or third I had no idea. It wasn't till much later when I watched the race back that I realised how hard Sandra and me pushed each other to the tape. I certainly didn't know I had broken the World Record until someone on the track told me and I remember saying 'Me?' When I heard that, it was like time being switched back on, and I realised where I was and what I had done. I had been so concerned with winning I hadn't even thought about a World Record and it just shocked me to find myself in that position.

CJ: Wow. Winning under those circumstances is incredible, and keeping quiet about the flu, meant no-one knew what you were dealing with out there!

SG: No and so I learnt so much about myself that day and out of all my races, that one gave me the most pleasure because I learnt what I could do when I wasn't 100%, how much I could push myself and what sort of character I had. It was just like wow! Gosh that is unbelievable and I shocked myself, and what I learnt was that not everything has to be 100% right physically, and that if your mind is right you can talk yourself into situations and then anything can happen.

CJ: So it can!

SG: Any way I think after all that I deserve another cream cake.

Sally Gunnell OBE

Medals at major championships

Olympic Games

GOLD	1992	Barcelona	400mH
BRONZE	1992	Barcelona	4 x 400m relay

World Championships

GOLD	1993	Stuttgart	400mH
SILVER	1991	Tokyo	400mH
BRONZE	1993	Stuttgart	4 x 400m relay

European Championships

GOLD	1994	Helsinki	400mH

European Cup

GOLD	1989	Gateshead	400m
GOLD	1991	Frankfurt	400mH
GOLD	1993	Rome	400mH
GOLD	1994	Birmingham	400mH

Commonwealth Games for England

GOLD	1986	Edinburgh	400mH
GOLD	1990	Auckland	400mH
GOLD	1990	Auckland	4 x 400m relay
GOLD	1994	Victoria	400mH
GOLD	1994	Victoria	4 x 400m relay
SILVER	1990	Auckland	100mH

Personal best

100mH	12.82	1988
400mH	52.74	1993

b. 29th July 1966. Chigwell, Essex.

Mrs. Bigg, Sally's married name, seems to suit her since she held the Grand Slam of Olympic, World, Commonwealth and European titles as well as the World record all at the same time!

Sally was an accomplished athlete and came to the hurdle event after achieving a certain amount of success in the long jump, pentathlon and notably the 100mH where she won the Commonwealth Games title in 1986 in Edinburgh. Once she adjusted to the 400mH she made the event her own and fought some memorable battles notably with Sandra Farmer-Patrick of the US. Sally's first Olympics came in Seoul in 1988 where she finished fifth – but more importantly, in a personal best time of 54.03s.

In Auckland in 1990 she took her second Commonwealth gold this time in the 400mH and then in 1991 took silver at the Tokyo World Championships. Despite her disappointment her time set a new personal best and a new national record of 53.16s.

Sally was selected as the British women's team captain for the 1992 Barcelona Olympics, and her expectations were high. It turned out to be a disappointing games for the British athletes, however Sally delivered on her potential and took her rival Sandra Farmer-Patrick on the home bend to keep her lead till the finish. It was only the fifth Olympic track and field medal won by a British woman, as she followed in the footsteps of Mary Rand, Ann Packer, Mary Peters and Tessa Sanderson. The British public took Sally to their hearts, and she was a shining light during what was a golden era for British Athletics.

The following year, 1993, was World Championship year and Sally was determined that this was her race. The record books show she took gold in the 400m hurdles in Stuttgart, breaking the world record as she did so. The story behind her experience at the championships is a remarkable triumph of mind over matter. Her world record lasted for two years before it was beaten by Kim Batten of the US, but it remains the British record, at 52.74s.

Sally hadn't had much success at the European Championships; she had been eliminated in the heat of the 100m hurdles in 1986, and had finished sixth in the 400m hurdles final in 1990. Her form in 1994 was red hot and her winning run was only interrupted by a loss to Kim Batten of the US, a defeat Sally quickly revenged beating Kim at the Goodwill Games. The European Championships in Helsinki would give her the Grand Slam of titles, and she cruised through the final, beating Silvia Rieger by over a second.

Sally defended her Commonwealth 400m hurdles title in Victoria in 1994, and set a new Games record of 54.51sec. She also won a second gold medal when she anchored England's 4 x 400m relay team to victory, repeating the double gold medal performance she achieved at the previous Commonwealth Games.

She was ranked number one in the world in 1991, 1992, 1993 and 1994. She defended her Olympic title in Atlanta in 1996, but injury struck and the following year Sally announced her retirement.

Sally has a successful and varied TV career and is in high demand as a motivational speaker and facilitator of creative business development and motivational programmes.

www.sallygunnell.com

Steve Cram

"It's hard to go even harder when you are already flat out – but I did."

I love competition, and Steve against Said Aouita was the best race I have ever seen in my life. Sally Gunnell against Sandra Farmer-Patrick in the World Championships of 1993 came close, but Steve Cram against Said Aouita in Nice, in 1985, was the ultimate race for me.

I work alongside Steve on the BBC athletics coverage, and I am always impressed and surprised by the depth of his knowledge of records and times, even when it comes to marathons – it's nearly as good as mine! But when you see someone so often the danger is you forget just how good they were. I don't with Steve – he was brilliant. He was absolutely brilliant.

I have a feeling though he may have given up most, if not all his athletic medals and achievements, for one appearance in the red and white of Sunderland Football Club and to hear the Roker Roar as he broke the back of the net with a 30 yard winner in the Premiership, or the F.A Cup final, against say . . . Newcastle or Middlesbrough.

Steve you are in this book just for your sheer brilliance.

CJ: Steve when you broke onto the scene you were going into an arena dominated by Steve Ovett and Sebastian Coe! Was that . . . daunting?

SC: Initially it was a great bonus because we hadn't had much success in Britain over middle distance in the 1970s. Brendan Foster and Dave Bedford were doing the long distance, and Brendan incidentally was the first big influence on me. When I was fourteen I can remember going to see Seb Coe run as a junior, I had read about him in *Athletics Weekly* magazine, and I went to see him race in Nottingham and I was rather excited and looking around thinking which one is he? And when I saw him I thought 'what that little one there!?'

But he was a big name even then, as he was breaking junior records, so he was setting targets for me a runner, and I was four years behind him. So Steve Ovett and Seb Coe began to raise the profile of the middle distance events when I began to break through at the age of about seventeen. One thing I remember is that both of them were very willing to give advice and Steve Ovett in particular was happy to talk with me, and give me his time, as was his coach Harry Wilson. But early on, no, it wasn't daunting – most importantly for me was seeing British athletes winning at major championships and breaking world records, that painted a clear picture in my mind that even if you are from Britain – you can do this! Later on it got a bit tougher because I had to try and beat them!

CJ: So they really helped engage you in athletics.

SC: Oh yes, but I was not the only one. There was a whole bunch of us, in my age group all being inspired by what those two were doing, which made it very, very competitive! My great rival was Graham Williamson from Glasgow a real tough nut, and he and I would regularly trade wins and records, and in fact for the European Junior Championships in 1979 I decided to switch to the 3000m to avoid Graham because he had beaten me twice that year and knew I would inevitably end up being the second best 1500m junior runner in Europe that year! As I expected Graham won gold in the 1500m, and he still holds the European Junior record for the mile by the way, remarkable! I won gold in the 3000m at those Junior Championships as I had hoped. Like you Colin, Graham and I were at that time – the best in the junior world.

CJ: Can you remember the early days of racing Coe and Ovett?

SC: I do remember and that was one heck of an experience which I will never forget. I remember just after the Moscow Olympics, in a race at Crystal Palace in 1981, I came up on Steve Ovett's shoulder with 150 metres to go. I can remember hesitating, and thinking 'well there is no way I can go past the legend that is Steve Ovett!' Steve then kicked and won by about thirty metres! But from that point on I decided I couldn't be scared of either of them, or of their reputations, and although they were on top of their game that year, by the following year I was thinking about myself as almost being at their level. Seb then got injured or didn't run very well and Steve Ovett had run into some church railings so he missed all of 1982, and in the European Championships in 1982 I finally won my first medal. But it wasn't till 1984 that all three of us raced against each other.

CJ: In 1983 came the inaugural World Championships. That was an important period in your career.

SC: I was incredibly excited at the prospect. The Olympics had been boycotted in 1976 and 1980 and we almost knew there was another boycott coming in 1984, so this first World Championship promised to be the first time since 1968 where the best in the world would be together at a major championship. I had beaten Seb at a race in Gateshead, and he then pulled out of those World Championships, but Ovett was still going. I think a lot of people thought it was coming to the end of the Coe and Ovett dominance.

So there were quite a few athletes hungry for success, and hoping to take over their mantle if you like. Mike Boit of Kenya and John Walker of New Zealand were still around and Steve Scott of the US was getting close to the world record, and then there was a guy we had never heard of before the start of that year called Said Aouita, of Morocco. I had never raced him, but he was heading up the world rankings, and he was the one I was most nervous about in 1983 but I was gunning for the title. I knew I was in great shape and I did have the gold medal on my mind.

CJ: Does hindsight give the real situation a slightly more positive spin?

SC: Why don't you believe me?

CJ: I mean you sound like a very confident young athlete saying that the gold medal was on the cards for you – or does time fade the memory!!

SC: I know what you are saying, but no, I really was feeling that good, my form was good I was positive – I was in a good place mentally. Look, any young athlete has to believe, and I went into that year with my sights firmly set on wining that World title. I certainly felt I had as good a chance as anybody, and in a 1500m race there are certain things you have to do at certain times – or you just are not going to win the race. Your thought process already has to be ahead of yourself, that is vital. So in my head I had a plan of how to win the race, you just cannot go into races thinking 'Oh I hope everything goes right for me today'. OK, your plan may not work out, but you must have a plan and decide to execute that plan.

CJ: Would you say that to any young middle distance runner? That is slightly alien to me Steve because it's different to my event. I am not saying you can't plan in the 110mH, but it really is you, in your lane, against the hurdles, and there is very little you can do in terms of tactics of how to take on your competitors. It's more of a plan of how you are going to run your own race, and often the key is to run that irrespective of where everyone else is, you can't let that affect you.

SC: Of course. It's about going out there to try and be the best and to try and win, and to do that you must be prepared take hold of the specific situation in hand. I always believed that in my events you must make and take decisions that will win you the race. You can't just hope that you end up coming first, you must be completely aware of all that is going on around you, and be ready and alert to react to the changing situation in the race. You have to take the bull by the horns as it were! Any coach worth his or her salt will be telling athletes that. I would hope.

CJ: So you weren't . . . frightened as you lined up for the start, in the company of so many world class contenders for that title?

SC: Hahaha, no I honestly wasn't frightened, but I was apprehensive put it like that. I was certainly anxious about Said Aouita. I can tell you a story, we had been in the same semi final and I came alongside him up the home straight, and you know, I decided to put on a bit of a surge – just to see what he had – and there was a good response from him and I thought wooowww! But I had got a bit of inside information from his team that he didn't think he could out-kick the field or that he couldn't leave it late at least and therefore he would go hard from about 600 metres out, and try and win it from there. Now that suited me just fine so long as I could be close enough to him at that stage, so I was going into the race ready for those tactics.

CJ: I remember the first lap, you were . . . last! At the back bobbing along, with an afro!

SC: Was it an afro – or a mullet at that time?

CJ: Frizzy. Shocking. Whatever!

SC: Yes. Well any road, I jogged around at the back, Brendan Foster in commentary called it a 'gentlemanly pace', 70 odd seconds for the first 400 metres if I remember rightly. But I looked after myself, kept out of trouble, and moved up to be ready when the fireworks started. With 800 metres to go Aouita begins to work his way to the front on the outside, so I track him, follow him, and the adrenalin is raging now with the anticipation of what was about to happen, it was about to all kick off. So as I was expecting, with 600 metres to go Said moves out and kicks hard. Steve Ovett isn't ready for that and is boxed in right at the back of the field, but I am right behind Aouita. So I kick hard to follow his break. So the next part of my plan was to stay with him, till about 300 metres to go.

CJ: When you say he kicked, how fast are you going?

SC: Well I can't speak for Aouita – but I can promise you Colin I am going absolutely flat out, top gear, so I would hope he was going absolutely flat out as well! I mean I was going flat out just to stay with him.

CJ: Wow, and by then the crowd knew this was the business part of the race!

SC: Yes and the noise of the crowd almost drowned out the noise of the race, you know the breathing, the noise of the spikes on the track.

CJ: Nicole Cooke our Olympic road race cycling champion, once told me, that she liked having a noisy crowd at the finish of stages because it meant she couldn't hear her own breathing, as sometimes the sound of that under all the effort scared her. It's a great picture she put in my mind. So you are flat out staying with Aouita.

SC: Yes and all the time I knew the others would be coming, and Steve Scott certainly was! He was timing his attack and winding it up! With 200 metres to go I had planned to go hard. It's hard to go harder when you are already flat out – but I did. I was absolutely flying around that top bend. At that stage you can't be sure whether your plan will work out, or whether someone is going to come past – and then you would have to ask yourself again whether there was any last ounce left in your tank. So, as to plan, I kept that pace going as well as I could, and the line seemed to be edging closer, and closer. I knew Steve Scott would be coming, but very soon down that home straight I realised that I was clear and just had to keep it going to the tape.

CJ: I can remember it being massive news back home in Britain, on the TV, was it your best race?

SC: I do cite that race as the way to run a 1500m race; it was, tactically, a very well executed race plan. It would have been more traditional for me, and less painful I might add, to have stayed on Aouita's shoulder, till we came off the final bend and try to take him there, but, looking back I would have been caught on the line by Steve Scott. That's why my race plan worked. Going early put me out of reach of Steve Scott's finish, and although he was finishing strongly, I was away and clear, and he must have known that quite early on, and realised he wasn't going to catch me.

Yes it was seen by a huge global TV audience, and up till then I had been the promising lanky Northerner, yes with frizzy hair Colin, but from then on I seemed to have been accepted by the public as a quality distance runner capable of challenging for major titles – and worth watching on the telly! It was quite a feeling to read articles now about the rivalry between Seb Coe, Steve Ovett . . . and Steve Cram.

CJ: Let's talk World Records because my favourite race of all time, of any race at any championship, was the 1500m race in the Nice Grand Prix, July 1985, when three runners seemed to want to put one over each other. Did you go out aiming to break the world record?

SC: Aye what a night that was! Ironically neither Said Aouita nor I were going into that race looking for a world record. The race had been set up with a pace maker for Joaquim Cruz, who had won the 800m at the 1984 Los Angeles Olympics the previous year, and everyone thought he would make a fantastic 1500m runner. Said Aouita had won the Olympic 5000 metres and I had unfortunately finished second behind Seb Coe in the 1500 metres! So it was all about Cruz, along with Aouita and me coming together in the first big race of the year. Now Cruz was a fantastic athlete, but he just went in at the deep end because both Said and I were ready and up for it that year. So when I heard what the pace maker was going to set for him I thought oh my gosh! That sounds a little ambitious but hey lets go with it. But Cruz went out the back door after about 1000 metres and we reached the bell at something like 2′36″ or something like that. So I thought well there is no world record here – but now I want to win this race.

Bang! Off I went, kick hard, keep it going, kick hard again with 200 metres to go, and I can hear the crowd screaming so I knew Said was coming, I knew he would be close – I didn't think he would be that close mind! With 30 metres to go I could hear him, you know I could hear his footsteps I could feel his presence, and I was hanging on, hanging on and the line seemed an awful long way away. So when I crossed the line I looked at the time and saw 3′29″, a new world record, and I thought no way!

I had run a 53″ last lap which wasn't how records were broken. You usually had a quick race and tried to hang on till the tape. Both Said and I had broken the 3′30″ barrier and I had shaved over a second off Steve Ovett's record, when we hadn't planned it.

CJ: Did you celebrate that night – I mean you were in Nice in July!?

SC: Colin I can assure you that night was a great night, I went to doping control and because I didn't want to hang around there I drank a few beers – only because it is a good diuretic and makes you pee. From there we went on to have a few more . . . and ended up in a bar in Nice somewhere, goodness knows where, with Said Aouita up on stage playing drums and me playing guitar – or was it the other way around – that's where my memory gets a little fuzzy Colin.

CJ: You had to let your hair down sometimes Steve. What do you love about the 1500 metres?

SC: Where do I start! What I particularly love is a tactical middle distance race. Today we see far too many loaded races where it is a bit of a procession to extract a fast time. The pace maker sets it up, the pack trudge around after him, and its a bun fight at the end. 'In my day' some people would say that the pace was slow – but I loved that. You could see people having to work out tactics, like, should I go now, should I kick, where is 'so and so'. It was like cat and mouse, and it produced some memorable races for those reasons, not for a fast time – but because it was like chess! You could literally see people wilting under the pressure. That's why I like watching the IAAF World Championships because you do tend to get a better tactical race with less emphasis on the race against the clock.

CJ: What does the future of British athletics hold?

SC: It inspires me to see certain things, like when we have the day of the Great North Junior Run, up here in Newcastle and Gateshead. We have thousands of kids turning out, and there are hundreds and thousands of people coming out to run fun runs like the Great North Run all over Britain – it's fantastic to see. It really is great to see so many people enjoying athletics. Because that's what it is – its fun athletics.

However! However Colin! Not many or at least not enough of those fun runners are then going on to join athletic clubs, and maybe dipping their toe into a more competitive environment. I am sure some would find that they enjoyed that competitive environment and I am sure some would be very good! You won't know how good you are, or how good you could be, until you take the first steps towards testing yourself out. So the clubs and the governing bodies have to do something better to make athletics more attractive for people to do that.

Now without being too negative about it, that has to happen – urgently! We do need some fairly radical changes, mostly within the clubs but also within the majority of schools. I think that is the only way that we will have the numbers involved at the grass roots of the sport, and that could lead us to a situation where we are seeing British athletes once again competing for medals at a world level. Imagine having a situation again where British athletes are competing against each other, for the major medals and the world records just like Ovett, Coe and someone called Steve Cram did many moons ago.

CJ: Winning world championships, breaking world records, would you say it was like a dream come true for you Steve? I mean when you poured over *Athletics Weekly* all those years ago, that was what you dreamt of at night right?

SC: I don't know about that, yes I did read *Athletics Weekly* with huge interest. But, no. To say it was a dream come true would not be strictly correct. When I was fifteen or sixteen I don't think I ever dreamt that I would win an athletic World Championship, it's not like playing in an F.A Cup Final for Sunderland – which I genuinely did dream about.

CJ: No-one would dream about that!

SC: I did Colin! Many, many times. Still do!

CJ: Do you wake up in a cold sweat?

SC: No I usually wake up just as I am climbing the steps at Wembley to receive the F.A Cup! I've already scored the winner, but I never seem to get that cup in my hands!

CJ: You should give them a ring, they may want to recruit you even in your old age!

SC: Don't now Colin!! Back when I was a teenager, yes, there was an obviously huge aspiration to develop as an athlete, and to be the best I could possibly be, and I guess that ultimately would involve winning a World Championship or breaking a World Record. So the sense of achievement when that did happen was absolutely immense.

I did actually say in an interview – when I was asked what did it feel like to break a world record – that it was 'like as if Sunderland had won the F.A Cup!' Now I admit that wasn't the most insightful comment to anyone who doesn't know football in the North East, but that's how I felt. I felt like a kid. I felt like it was Christmas and birthdays all rolled into one.

I remember when Sunderland did win the cup in 1973. I felt like it was the best thing that ever would happen to me. And I think that's how I felt when successes came my way in athletics – that this could be the best thing that ever happens in my athletics career.

CJ: So maybe I can say that you lived the dream?

SC: Yes I lived the dream, and all those years of fun and hard work and sacrifices by people around me – and all the reasons why I did the sport – all come together in moments like that, and they may never ever be surpassed – and for that reason they remain very, very special.

CJ: Steve. Thanks. Great memories.

Steve Cram MBE

Medals at major championships

Olympic Games

SILVER	1984	Los Angeles	1500m

World Championships

GOLD	1983	Helsinki	1500m

European Championships

GOLD	1982	Athens	1500m
GOLD	1986	Stuttgart	1500m
BRONZE	1986	Stuttgart	800m

Commonwealth Games for England

GOLD	1982	Brisbane	1500m
GOLD	1986	Edinburgh	1500m
GOLD	1986	Edinburgh	800m

Personal best

800m	1.42.88	1985
1500m	3.29.67	1985
Mile	3.46.32	1985

b. 14th October 1960. Jarrow, Tyneside.

Steve Cram proved his potential as a talented youngster when he won the European Junior 3000m title in 1979.

The 'Jarrow Arrow' went on to realise that early potential and remains the UK record-holder over the mile, 1500m and 2000m. His duals with Steve Ovett and Sebastien Coe constituted a period in British middle distance running history, which may never be surpassed in terms of the passion and profile they generated around the world.

During the summer of 1985 he set world records at 1500m, 2000m and the mile distance in a nineteen day period. His four successive victories at the Oslo Dream Mile were watched by huge audiences back in the UK.

Following an unsuccessful appearance at the 1980 Moscow Olympic Games he made his breakthrough at the 1982 Commonwealth Games where he won the 1500m title beating New Zealand's John Walker and Kenya's Mike Boit. He soon backed this up with the European title in the same year at Athens.

The World Championships in Helsinki in 1983 saw Steve beat a class field including Said Aouita and Steve Ovett, to become the inaugural champion, and this gave expectation for him to do well at the 1984 Olympic Games in Los Angeles. However his season was interrupted by injury and he chased Sebastien Coe home in the Olympic 1500m final to win silver.

In 1985 his season really took off as he beat Joaquim Cruz, the reigning Olympic 800m champion, in 1.42.88s, Steve's fastest ever time for his least favourite event. He also became the first man ever to run 1500m in under 3.30s, after a great tussle with Said Aouita in Nice. In front of his home fans in Gateshead he became the second fastest man in history over 1000m in a time of 2.12.88s. This was probably the most memorable period for British middle distance running, when records were broken in a summer which will be remembered for Steve going for home from the bell.

His two medal haul at the 1986 Edinburgh Commonwealth Games saw him win gold at the 1500m, and also beat off the challenge of

Tom McKean of Scotland and Peter Elliot of England in the 800m, to win in a time of 1.43.22s which is still a Commonwealth Games record today.

His season also included bronze at the European Championships in Stuttgart over 800m where Coe and Tom McKean took gold and silver for a British clean sweep. Steve stormed to victory at the 1500m where he beat Seb Coe into second place.

The one medal that eluded him was an Olympic Gold, and injury blighted his attempt at the Seoul Games in 1988 where he finished fourth in the 1500m.

Steve retired in 1994.

He is a regular athletics commentator for BBC Sport

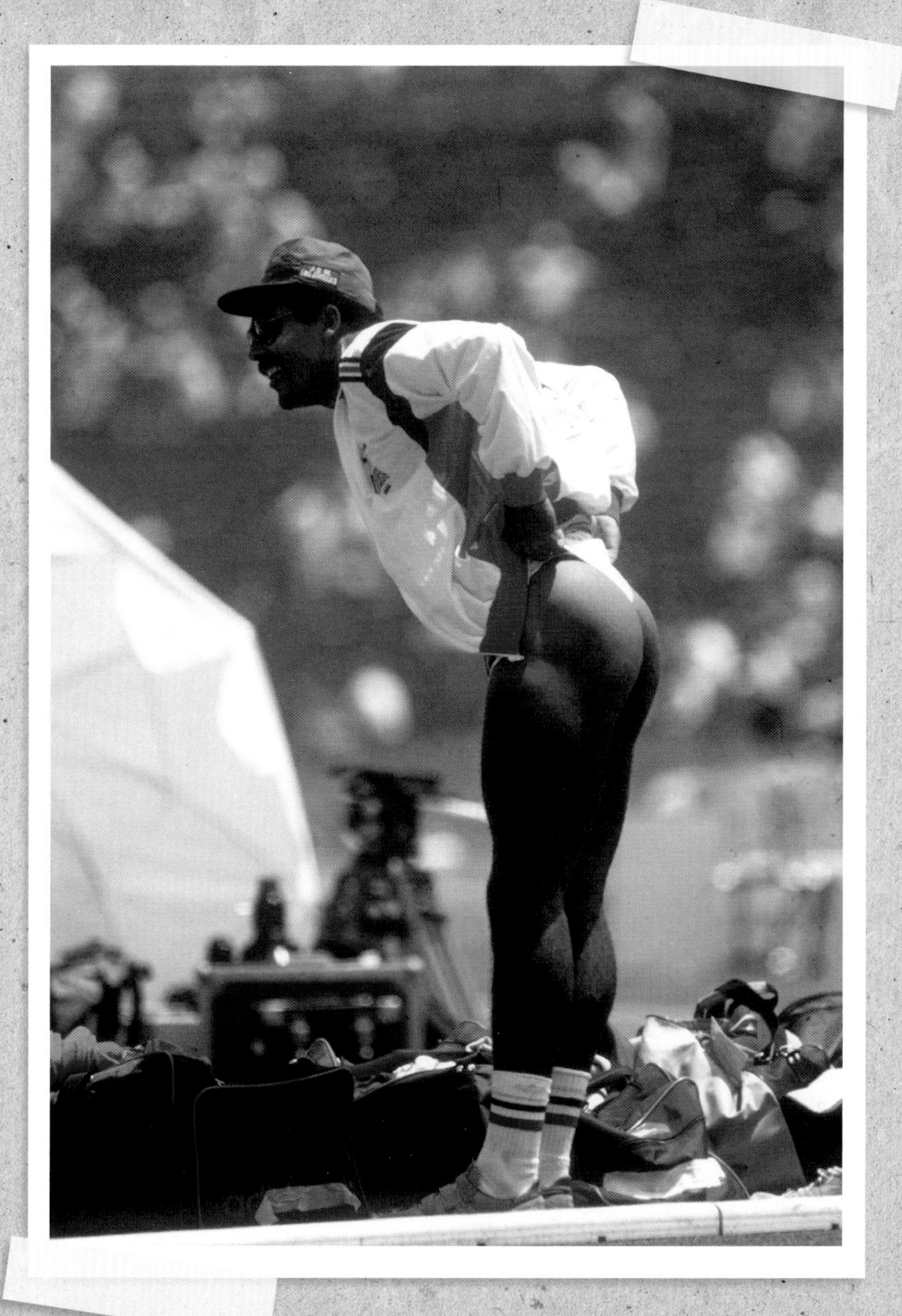

Daley, always had a smile, usually on his face!

Action Images / Sporting Pictures

Allan Wells wins the 100m Olympic title in Moscow by the thickness of his vest!

Bob Thomas/Getty Images

Yep I am afraid that is another world record. it just is. Jonathan. World Champs 1995. Gothenburg.

Mike Powell/ALLSPORT

Daley on form!
Allan, down crouch and go!
JE on yer bike

Oscar, a fairy and a space cadet in Beijing '08

Action Images

Tessa the Golden Girl with Fatima - who's the cheekiest?

Chris Smith/Getty Images

Sally finally realizes she is '93 World Champion. Sandra FP already knows it.

Action Images

Oscar in the blocks

Tessa loves Ali more than she loves me!!

Nice cherries Sally!

Sheer brilliance Steve despite the frizzly hair. Helsinki '83

Bob Thomas/Getty Images

Mum, Dad and me were in tears at this point. Don. Montreal Olympics.

James Drake /Sports Illustrated/Getty Images

Fatima and the difference between winning. . . . and not.

Action Images / Sporting Pictures / Tony Marshall

Steve still waiting for a call from Sunderland FC!!

Water for my dry mouth! With Don.

Sport was my saviour. Fatima.

Captain Courageous. Old Man Akabusi. Two chest Regis. pretty boy Black. Tokyo '91

Action Images

Steve 'King Competitive' Backley

Action Images / Richard Heathcote

David Hemery storms to a golden world record. Mexico City '68

Rolls Press/Popperfoto/Getty Images

Bang. Boom. Feeoo. Feeoo. Bosh. Akabusi.

The blind squirrel with Steve B!

The first satellite sportsman David Hemery

Don Quarrie

"It's the anticipation that makes the experience so worth while."

I pride myself on my time keeping – after all, time management was always an important part of my life for so many years – but I found myself very early for my arranged meeting with Don. Strange that! I know him well from the years we both have spent on the athletics circuit, but I find I have butterflies in my stomach and a slightly dry mouth, and I keep checking my watch – although he isn't late. It's me that's early. One of my earliest childhood memories is of being in our front room, in Cardiff, with my Dad and Mum and sister watching his pursuit of the sprint double in the 100m and 200m, at the Montreal Olympics in 1976. My parents hadn't been in Britain all that long, having come from Jamaica, so they were really passionate about Don as he was a sporting icon in Jamaica. Like most Jamaicans, my parents were very noisy and it was perfectly clear they wanted him to win so badly! They were very vocal, not critical, but vocal in their support of Don. It made a huge impression on me. I thought, wow, if that was me out there they would be jumping up and down and bouncing off the walls and screaming for me in the same way! Don was quite small and fitted the David v Goliath script really well, where a good little un could beat a good big un – if the little un is good enough. Don was gracious both in victory and defeat, and when I got to know him years later, to me, he really was 'a gentleman of the track',

I order a glass of water to wet my mouth again, ok, and to calm my nerves!? What is this feeling!

DQ: Hi Colin, you are early!

CJ: Yes I am. You as always are exactly on time. Good to see you again.

DQ: Good to see you back home on The Island my friend!

CJ: Don I remember you coming to Swansea, in Wales, to hold a coaching clinic when I was about thirteen years old, and I got your autograph. Do you remember me that day?

DQ: No I do not Colin. Next question?

CJ: Hahaha . . . well I guess that's understandable. Can I take you back to the Montreal Olympics in 1976, which I followed at home in Cardiff on the TV – and I was in tears when you lost the 100m. My Dad and Mum had to console me. We were all so upset, I can still picture it now.

DQ: I thank you for your support, and had I known back then the intensity of your support, the result might well have been different Colin.

CJ: I doubt it. What do you remember of the events as they unfolded?

DQ: Well that moment, of crossing the line, in second place and losing the 100m final was a great disappointment to me; you know you lose a big race, you lose an Olympic Final, you are going to be hugely disappointed. As an athlete you work so hard to prepare, and there are also a lot of people who have assisted you in your career so you are also running for them. All my friends and family and supporters at home in the Caribbean they too were willing me to do well, so not to come away with success was going to be a painful experience, and one that every athlete bar none will experience at some stage in their career. I was actually leading at one stage, but could not hold on and eventually was beaten into silver place.

I must add that Hasely Crawford of Trinidad and Tobago, who took the gold medal, was a good friend of mine so in that respect I found I could deal with it a lot better, but there is no getting away from it, it was a race I was desperate to win, yes I wanted it, but I could not win it. So immediately after the race, in my mind I told myself 'You are not going to lose the 200m'. So I guess I switched off from the 100m immediately, and switched on to what was coming up, and I used all my mental effort to do that.

CJ: So did you take that to the blocks of the 200m?

DQ: I can honestly say that I never once thought of the 100m final after the race. I managed to leave it there. There were no emotions that I took forward. I was facing the danger of being swamped by the disappointment of the 100m and that would lose me the 200m. So I found that I ran all the heats of the 200m with a fresh purpose. I focussed myself to test my ability to run the bend to the best of my ability; to test my ability to lift myself; to test my ability to run the straight in the best way I ever had. In this way I could concentrate on different aspects of the 200m event. Staying positive and very focussed was the key thing. Even when I ended up in lane 2 in the final I told myself 'everything is fine with lane 2, everything is still just fine!' I had practised in my mind that I could end up in lane 1, so having lane 2 was just fine compared to that! So in my head I had done everything to make sure that I was in the right frame of mind to be able to win the 200m. Winning meant everything to me, especially under those circumstances.

CJ: That mental concentration is as great an attribute as the physical.

DQ: It is and I found I needed to work hard at it. The second the gun went in the final of the 200m, I took off and I knew when I hit the end of the curve that I would win. From there on it was just a matter of whether to take off or just hold it all steady and go for the victory. Now Millard Hampton from the US was closing a little, but I knew he could not take me because at one stage I gave a little surge to see what he had, and he did not come with me, so I knew that I could hold him off, and make sure of the victory – because winning was everything.

CJ: Well I remember how much we celebrated that day in our house, and that the way you came back after the disappointment of the 100m made a huge impression on me as a youngster. Seeing my Dad and Mum so excited about it was what led me into athletics. We see today a great rivalry between the sprinters of Jamaica and the US, but that rivalry was there in your day, and your rivalry with the American sprinter Steve Williams?

DQ: Yes it was a great rivalry, but also, oddly some might think, a friendly rivalry. I was training in the US at that time and I was studying and based in Southern California, so I had my supporters in the US as well as back home in the Caribbean and Steve Williams had his US based support so it made for a great environment. We used to assist each other from time to time. If I was able to beat Steve by a big margin off the curve in one race I would say to him afterwards 'Hey I killed you on the curve, you didn't run it the way you could have or should have', or if he was able to gain on me down the straight he would say so and we would talk. So indirectly we were helping each other improve, despite being rivals. There was no animosity between us, it was a positive rivalry and we made sure from time to time that no-one came in between us. If someone else beat one of us it became an issue and again in a similar way we would look at why that could happen, so we would teach each other about it. We knew every time we stepped out on the track that we would run fast, and we developed our rivalry to suit both of us, and I think that heightened the sprints a lot.

CJ: You certainly flied the flag for your countries.

DQ: Yes I was training in the US and they had great facilities, but I was still Jamaican and so when it came down to who would win a particular race it was Don Quarrie of Jamaica or Steve Williams of the US, so it did create a lot of excitement, and it did create a lot of publicity around the world not only for Steve and myself but, in my case, for the Island of Jamaica.

CJ: Today in athletics we have a delicious Jamaica versus America head to head situation in particular between Usain Bolt and Asapha Powell of Jamaica and Tyson Gay of the US.

DQ: Yes it is a great situation for Jamaica and for the sport of athletics, because the more world class head to heads you have, the better and more attractive the events are going to be. Maybe one race doesn't distinguish who the best is, but a series of head to heads does, and gives an audience great continuity to watch over a season. This raises the profile of the sport but also, I believe, the standards of the athletes.

CJ: How does it affect the Island of Jamaica?

DQ: Well it takes the name of Jamaica around the world, but more importantly it creates a buzz in Jamaica and emotions run high and the desire to be the best sprint nation in the world gets closer and stronger because youngsters come into the sport, and they come with an increased passion and desire. Colin you have been to the Jamaica High School Games yourself and seen the event that is the culmination of the season for our children in front of a wildly passionate packed stadium – and I am talking 35,000 people packed in there – to watch a high school event! So this offers our best young runners the opportunity to compete in a high pressure situation what with the crowds and the rivalry. It really does serve our talent development well, and we can see a crop of young talent every year, and we have to ensure that that vein of talent continues and is strengthened. I think the current group of successful male and female Jamaican sprinters shows the success of that system.

CJ: Usain Bolt came through that talent development system, and he took your Jamaican 200m record.

DQ: Well Colin I have often said over the years that it has taken far too long to break that record so I was very happy when Usain took it finally, because for Jamaica to be at the top we need athletes running sub 20 seconds for the 200m. I was not surprised when Usain broke it as I thought he could run low 19 seconds for the 200m – and for the record I think he can run low 44 seconds for the 400m. There is more to come from Usain, and by that I am not saying I am putting expectations upon him – just that his development is showing these signs and that he will lead us to those sorts of times.

CJ: Who inspired you then?

DQ: I would say my idol was a Jamaican sprinter Lennox Miller who passed away a few years back. I watched him at high school when I was fourteen or so, and I thought 'oh I want to be like him.' After high school I was fortunate that I had him around a lot of the time to motivate me. I looked up to what he had achieved and other Jamaican athletes as well, and I was always respectful, and I listened to what they told me because I recognised that not everyone was willing to hand on information to assist other athletes. I used it to better myself and I still keep in touch with some of those guys today. I remember at the time Lennox called me 'son' and he was like a father to me. The word is respect. I had it for Lennox and that helped me a lot.

CJ: Is there any advice you can offer to youngsters?

DQ: Simply go to some track and field meets, make the effort, you may meet some of the stars, and if you do I would hope they are gracious and take the time to sign an autograph or offer a few words of encouragement – that should be in the remit of any athlete who is great in his sport, the respect for the future of the sport and the important role the high profile athletes have in securing that future. And if you can, go see a sprint head to head, even on the TV, because for me, it's experiencing the 'anticipation' of a great race that entertains the crowds, and the youngsters in the crowd – and that brings out our future athletes.

CJ: You were a great inspiration to countless children in Jamaica and to myself here in Wales. You certainly inspired me towards my own career. Thank you for your company, good to see you again DQ.

DQ: Thank you for those kind words Colin. I really have enjoyed the chat. What was the cause of your arriving so early my friend?

CJ: Anticipation?

Don Quarrie

Medals at major championships

Olympic Games

GOLD	1976	Montreal	200m
SILVER	1976	Montreal	100m
SILVER	1984	Los Angeles	4 x 100m relay
BRONZE	1980	Moscow	200m

Pan American Games

GOLD	1971	Cali	100m
GOLD	1971	Cali	200m

Commonwealth Games for Jamaica

GOLD	1970	Edinburgh	100m
GOLD	1970	Edinburgh	200m
GOLD	1970	Edinburgh	4 x 100m relay
GOLD	1974	Christchurch	100m
GOLD	1974	Christchurch	200m
GOLD	1978	Edmonton	100m

Personal best

100m	10.07 sec	1976
200m	19.86 sec	1971

b. 25th February 1951. Kingston, Jamaica.

Don Quarrie is a Jamaican sprint legend who competed in five Olympic Games, which is a remarkable achievement in any event, but especially for a sprinter.

During his early days he made a huge impact as a schoolboy sprinter at Camperdown High School, Jamaica, winning sprint titles in each class at Boys Championships. Remarkably he made the 1968 Jamaican Olympic team as a 17 year old schoolboy, but injured himself during training and had to withdraw.

He moved to the United States and studied at the University of Southern California, where he graduated with a degree in Business and Public Administration, and took full advantage of the facilities and the coaching methods there, to further his development as an athlete.

Don stepped onto the international scene with a sprint triple at the 1970 Commonwealth Games winning gold in the 100m, the 200m as well as the 4 x 100m relay. Don's association with these Games is written in history for he became the first man to win six Commonwealth Gold medals. He won three consecutive 100m titles, and at the Christchurch, New Zealand Games in 1974 was the first man to successfully defend both the 100m and 200m titles.

His Olympic dreams began with disappointment at the 1972 Olympic Games in Munich, where he decided, due to injury, to contest only one event, and chose the 200m. He progressed well through the preliminary rounds yet despite his original injury being to the ligaments of his right knee, he collapsed half way through the semi final race with a pulled muscle in his left leg, and had to be carried from the track on a stretcher. He returned four years later to the Olympics, highly determined to do well, since in the mean time he had achieved number one world ranking status in 1975 for both sprint distances. The 1976 Montreal Olympics were to be his finest hour capturing the silver medal in the 100m and gold in the 200m which was Jamaica's first Olympic gold medal since the 1952 Games in Helsinki where George Rhosen and Herb McKenley finished first and second in the 400m.

Don resumed his love affair with the Olympics in 1980 where he won two more medals in Moscow, a bronze in the 200m and silver in the 4 x 100m relay. He competed at his fifth Olympic Games in Los Angeles in 1984 but whilst he did not medal in the individual sprints, he won silver with the Jamaican relay team, finishing just behind the United States.

Don tied for the 200m world record in 1971 at the Pan American Games in Cali, Columbia, with a blistering 19.83s hand timing, with an unofficial electronic timing of 19.86s. In 1975 he again tied the 200m world record, with 19.8s and also tied the 100m record with a hand-timed mark (9.9s) in 1976, thus becoming one of only a few athletes to have held these records simultaneously.

Fatima Whitbread

"Sport was my Saviour."

We arrived at Fatima's house on a hot sunny afternoon and found her, relaxed, in her beautiful garden surrounded by the aroma of fresh flowers and of a newly mowed [and stripped] lawn. She was prepared, as always, with fresh orange juice, iced and ready.

Each of my icons has their own story of how they reached the top of their sport, and for me Fatima's is ' If you don't at first succeed, try, try again'. Fatima had to pick herself up and dust herself down many a time. I remember when she lost the World Championship in Helsinki in '83 to Tina Lilak's last throw of the final, it was evidently devastating and Fatima was on the ground in tears. It was absolute drama for everyone watching at home, but I know how Fatima felt, and I know how difficult it is to pick yourself up and move on from something like that. So when I saw her nail the world record in Stuttgart, in the European Championships 1986 it was just unbelievable. I was so pleased.

Fatima today is looking slim and fit, almost petite, which is quite a contrast to her competing days when as a muscular pocket battleship she hurled the javelin ridiculous distances. Fatima was one of the first female super stars of the modern sporting era of the 1980s and definitely one of my sporting icons. Fatima I so admire your persistence.

These days everyone gets so excited about Beyonce shaking her bootie – well that is so dated – the Whitbread wiggle was around a long time ago.

CJ: Well Fatima it's been a long time and we haven't caught up for so long . . . but back in the day I can remember I used to watch you out there, competing, and I always had the impression you were . . . well . . . as hard as nails. Is there really a soft side to Fatima Whitbread?!?

FW: Colin of course there is a soft side. As an athlete you need to be really tough. To compete against the best in the world there is no point having too soft a nature, you have got to have a tough side to you. But if the truth be known there is a soft side to me, and part of that comes out in my creativity – and my love of design, as an interior designer. I have just finished doing my own home for the second time!

CJ: It is beautiful; I can't believe what you have managed to do with your own bare hands! It looks superb – what do you love most?

FW: I love the plasma room, where I can relax with my friends. It's a big house so it took me nine months to go all through. The hallway alone took me three weeks to strip it of all the wallpaper and I went through three wallpaper strippers! Then preparing the surface pointing all the cracks and holes then sanding them back – there was so much dust here, but the preparation was worth it and with the ceiling lamps and the cornices, and the decor I love how it all turned out.

CJ: In your 'former life' as I like to call mine, as an athlete, did you find yourself being selfish?

FW: Well you have to be selfish to succeed and to achieve great things, in any sphere of life you need to be – or a certain amount of you has to be – selfish, in order to go ahead and concentrate 100% on what you are doing. For me it was no different – training seven days a week, three times a day and having to change my whole lifestyle and mindset to pursue what I wanted to achieve. I also had to endure a tremendous amount on the diet side let alone the training side. There was enormous self-discipline I had to undergo, to get up and go out and prepare my whole body so that I could just chuck a javelin spear as far as I could! I am a kind and considerate person – or I would like to consider myself as being that! But when it comes to competing and succeeding yes there is a side to me that can be completely selfish, and I assume that all champions in athletics must have that. Don't we?

CJ: I would expect you to have said that you were selfish – but I agree there is another side to you. In 1993 at the World Championships, the night before my final you came to my room to pay me a visit and to give me some words of wisdom. You told me to take my opportunity and that it could be my day, if I really wanted it. I remember you spoke very softly and were very measured, and it must have been good because I went out and performed very well and won the World title, and broke the World record! So I see you as an inspiring and motivating person. Did you know you had that side to you?

FW: Mmmmm . . . I still remember that night as well, it did turn out well for you, and I was so, so happy for you. I think it's very important to remember, and you will know Colin since you have inspired a huge number of youngsters, once you become a figurehead, you need to be aware of the side of you that can help others. I mean dealing with the psychological approach to any major event is half the battle. The preparation, the training, the technical side is important, but the mental approach I think is all important and once you learn to understand yourself, as you and I did Colin – then you certainly know and recognise the pressures that can be bestowed upon others and what they need to do in order to deal with it. So yes you are in a position to help, and so maybe it comes naturally to be a motivator.

CJ: So who or what inspired you to be a javelin thrower?

FW: Initially it was Tessa Sanderson, I mean in the infancy of my career. After that there were a lot of inspirations for me . . . like Margaret Thatcher the then leader of the Conservative Party. She was a very strong leader and I admired her greatly for that. I guess Petra Felke as well because she came from the German Democratic Republic as it was then, and it was pretty tough there. They take kids from their families at a very young age and they have an institutionalised life whether they like it or not. Petra competed well and she wore it well and in competition she always brought the best out of me. So I respected her greatly and it was really nice to see her at the end win an Olympic title – once I had retired though!

CJ: Did you ever think that you would make such an impact upon the javelin event, because you really brought it on to be a talking point, and with that cheeky smile and the Fatima wiggle . . . can you still do that?

FW: Of course I can, although these days I have had to modernise with Run DMC, that's my party piece now!

CJ: But you did bring the event to life – did you ever think you would inspire so many!

FW: Well Colin, looking back Sport was my saviour. I mean because as a child – well I was abandoned as a baby. I don't mean put up for adoption, I mean abandoned as a baby, in a flat and it was only when the neighbours heard my cries that I was found. I then spent the next fourteen years in a children's home and I really was at the stage of what was it going to be for me? Academically I was too emotionally disturbed to concentrate much, you know I was fine but not an academic – but sport put me on an equal playing field. It gave me the confidence to succeed and to pursue the career that I chose, in track and field, and to go further and higher. So I guess from the age of 11 or 12 I knew I wanted to be a sports person, and to succeed meant everything to me. I mean you know in your mind – if you have set your heart on something, on being the best, you have got to live it. It's got to come from the heart. You have got to eat, drink and breathe what it is you want to do, and that has got to be your passion in life to succeed and to go all the way. If it isn't then it will be very hard to pick yourself up after any disappointment. For me that was most definitely the way forward through sport, and I actually ended up doing the javelin because I quite fancied David Ottley who was at that time the British record holder. My adopted mother

Margaret coached him so I decided to start throwing a few throws and that's why I took up the javelin.

CJ: Tessa Sanderson told me that a girl in her school first challenged her that she could beat her in the javelin on school sports day, so Tessa said 'no way' as Tessa would, and started practising and then went on to beat her! And that's how she started javelin. Tessa's reward was a bag of chips for a week bought for her by that girl.

FW: And she is still eating them! Sorry Tessa!

CJ: So for Tessa it was a challenge that inspired her, and I always find it interesting to hear what inspires you and how you achieve the ultimate because people often think that it's not every day circumstances that sets you off on the road to becoming a champion – but it is ultimately!

FW: Yes I agree, little things trigger them off, maybe an inspirational figure or a challenge. Then you have to realise your own dream, what it is that you would like to do, find your own niche in life. I found mine, I could express myself through sport. But you have got to have that passion and it's got to be self driven and it's got to come from the heart. Otherwise how else could I have come back from the disappointment of watching Tina Lilak win the 1983 World title with her last throw in Helsinki! It was like an absolute gut wrenching experience for me. That stadium was a lonely place, with Tina running all around the place and the crowd going crazy! A lonely place, and had I not absolutely loved my sport I think I could have easily given up there and then. But I do love it, so what do you do. You pick yourself up, dust yourself down, see if you can take the experience and make yourself stronger, and start over again.

CJ: That sounds like my Olympic experience in 1992! Now you were one of those rare people who set a world record during a major championship, tell me more about that.

FW: I guess a lot of the media and the written press were caught with their pants down – metaphorically speaking because it was very early in the morning during the qualifying rounds of the 1986 European Championships in Stuttgart. Nobody expected a world record throw there – least of all myself! I had been up all night the night before squatting those blasted mosquitoes that were keeping me awake – so I was ready for it! I just had to throw far enough to qualify for the next days final, so I was very relaxed, evidently in great shape and I threw 77.44m to set the record. So many people said to me afterwards 'oh you did it on the wrong day'!

CJ: Well I must admit I was worried for you – in my own mind I had this terrible, terrible headline of 'Fatima Whitbread world record holder – but still doesn't win the title!'

FW: Colin that sounds like a nightmare more like!

CJ: Well maybe it was a nightmare . . . did you dream the same nightmare!

FW: Well in a way it was a nightmare because every where I turned the media were there with the wink or the smile or the blowing of a kiss to the camera – which was what I did after my record throw. So I had to somehow come back down to earth and reproduce that form in the final to win, and no-one had really ever done that before. It really was a big ask for me but I believed in my abilities, I loved what I was doing . . . throwing the javelin, so I just went away in hiding and tried to keep a low profile. My mother Margaret, who was my coach, we tried not to get too excited about the record but to be honest it was emotionally draining. I mean Petra Felke, who was now the 'former' record holder, had qualified comfortably and I guess she was thinking 'right the pressure is now on you Whitbread!' It was a really tense time, and the press set it up as East verses West. But as you know Colin if you find yourself in that kind of form you just stay relaxed, let the technique work for yourself and ride the crest of the wave. Then there's no reason why you can't reproduce your performance, just as long as the pressure doesn't get to you.

CJ: So Fatima Whitbread, world record holder, takes the javelin, holds it high, and looks down the runway . . . what was the plan? Was there a plan!

FW: Well I thought to myself 'the responsibility I have today is to win.' But to do that obviously I would have to throw a long way because to beat someone of the calibre of Petra Felke – you couldn't do it with an average throw. So I was very tense but at the same time I was altogether focussed and ready, and as soon as I laced up my boots, stood on the runway with my spear aloft – I felt there was no stopping me. My first throw was only 62m or so, and it stuck in like a dart! Not a great start but I just knew there was more to come, although it must have been nerve racking for anyone watching, because Petra opened with a 72m throw, which would have won most titles! So although the pressure was really mounting from the word go, that is something you learn to live with. I guess I am a tough competitor and I threw 69m with my next attempt, which wan't long enough to trouble the leader. So the pressure must have been quite intense, but just keep control because my form was there I just had to wait for the right moment. Then, in the fourth round, I unleashed a 74m monster throw which flew on and on as I watched, it was a fantastic feeling watching it disappear into the sky!

But Felke still had one throw to go so I was a little bit nervous and I had to endure her last throw before knowing whether my throw had been enough to take the title. That seemed like an age.

CJ: And the history books show you had done enough to win. So realising dreams and making them your destiny is a fantastic experience – but then your dream really did turn into a nightmare as your athletic career was soon to be ended prematurely by injury . . . . .

FW: Yes too short Colin! Eight years too short! But then again there's a lot of young athletes who get injured and don't ever make an international team so I am thankful for the short lived career that I had. I certainly learned a lot about myself as a person, and it was great to meet and rub shoulders with the likes of you, and to learn about other people in the sport. We are all human beings after all and it's nice to know people and nice to work with different people and see how they tick and what sport does for them and how it creates their character under extreme pressure. I know at the time of my injury it was a huge blow but sitting here today, I can look back and see that it wasn't really. It made me move on, and made me set new challenges and we ended up setting up the Chatham 100 which was a sports marketing arm, and that ended up being a great learning curve.

CJ: Do you have any regrets; I mean you 'only' won Olympic silver, what was your medal tally anyway?

FW: Eleven major medals from different championships, I was World Champion, but never Commonwealth and, no Colin, never Olympic Champion. The year I should have won the Olympics I was unfortunately carrying the injury that ended my career, a ruptured rotator muscle.

CJ: It was your shoulder right?

FW: Yes a complete rupture of the shoulder muscle, and I don't think you can ever repair something back to as it was before. When you smash a cup or something you can stick it back with glue, but it will still have the cracks and scars – and in sport it's the same with injuries. But it comes with the territory, and for me that injury was the end of my career . . . and I never did get back.

CJ: That was a long pause! Did you ever think that something was missing? Did you ever think your career wasn't complete because it was cut short?

FW: Well I never had to make the decision of when to retire! But in my heart I would have liked to have had that decision to make. I would have retired in 1992. I could have won more titles, definitely the Olympics, the Commonwealths and probably one more World Title. But my dream was to break 80m which I believed was realistic.

CJ: Well Petra Felke went on to throw 80m . . .

FW: She did all credit to her. She was a great athlete and I think the two of us brought the best out of each other, and with Tina Lilak and Tessa Sanderson it was a great, great era for women's javelin.

CJ: So what about Fatima Whitbread these days then?

FW: Well I am very motivated because we have got London 2012 approaching – and it's not just London's games it's Britain's games and the next step is to try and get the youth as well as the whole nation motivated into a healthy way of life. Changing lifestyles and mindsets about the importance of winning is part of that and achieving a better quality of life for our young people.

CJ: You have a young son, Ryan, he is quite sporty – does he get that from your genes?

FW: Well we are all victims of our environment, or parts of our environment; I mean parents have a big influence on us – no doubt yours did Colin. So yes Ryan is quite sporty but also bright academically as well. Having said that you have to give them choices, help them to be rounded enough so when they reach that certain age they can move forward and make the right choices about what it is they want to do. I am not trying to beat the sport drum but I do think the right combination of sport and academic studies is a good healthy way of life and that's what we should aim for in young people today. Maybe the Olympic Games can help us achieve that in Britain and help youngsters realise their dreams and make them their destiny.

CJ: All the rewards, all the medals and honours you have won and been awarded – does one stand out?

FW: That's really hard because there are several different things that I have won that have meant so much to me for different reasons. In 1988 in the Seoul Olympics I shouldn't have been competing as I had a really bad illness and I should never have been there. I had only been throwing about 40m before the games but I took the chance and relied on my competitive spirit and came away with Olympic silver medal – and threw 70m! So that was my proudest moment. Yes definitely. But 1986 to 1987 was important to me because it was European Gold, World Gold and a World Record, so that was all very special. But I find it hard to single out one because they all have their special meaning and purpose to me.

CJ: You were awarded the BBC Sports Personality of the Year in 1987, that must have come as a nice surprise to you?

FW: Well you know what it's like Colin, everybody wants to be acknowledged for what they do and in sport it's a lot easier to get the accolades and the pats on the back than say in the commercial world. In a sporting arena there are times and distances that measure whether you have succeeded. So yes to have been chosen and awarded the BBC Personality of the Year was a fantastic achievement, it was the crème de la crème, and I was very touched that I had been chosen and it made me feel very proud. However at the same time it didn't pay any bills! I was still Fatima Whitbread who still had to go out the next year and start all over again – but it was nice to know that I had been acknowledged in that way and in those circumstances.

But I can tell you with hand on heart, that my proudest moment in life, if I have to be honest, amongst everything else, all the awards I have won, all the titles I have won and all the records I have ever broken – even if I had won 100 titles more Colin, it could not have come anywhere close to the birth of my son Ryan. That beats any gold medal there is. He is my pride and joy above anything I have ever achieved in Sport. I just hope he now has the opportunity to realise his own dream, and that he will be happy doing what he loves doing whatever that turns out to be.

CJ: I will drink to that, Fatima thank you and cheers.

FW: Cheers Colin come again soon.

CJ: Oh, by the way, where is the javelin you broke the world record with then?

FW: It's down the bottom of the garden, holding up my runner beans!

CJ: Get away!

FW: Come on come down and see it.

Fatima Whitbread MBE

Medals at major championships

Olympic Games

SILVER	1988	Seoul	Javelin
BRONZE	1984	Los Angeles	Javelin

World Championships

GOLD	1987	Rome	Javelin
SILVER	1983	Helsinki	Javelin

Commonwealth Games for England

SILVER	1986	Edinburgh	Javelin
BRONZE	1982	Brisbane	Javelin

European Championships

GOLD	1986	Stuttgart	Javelin

Personal best

Javelin	77.44 m	1986

b. 3rd March 1961. Stoke Newington, London.

Fatima came on the scene with a bang when she won the European Junior title in 1978 at the age of 18. She competed in the 1978 Commonwealth Games in Edmonton, finishing 6th in an event won by Tessa Sanderson. The guiding light behind her athletics career was the national javelin coach at that time Margaret Whitbread, although Margaret was much more than just a coach and mentor to Fatima. As a baby Fatima was left in a flat in north London by her biological mother, and was found after a few days by neighbours who heard her crying. She spent the next four months in hospital recovering from malnutrition. A desperately unhappy childhood saw her raised in children's homes until she came under the guidance of Margaret Whitbread, who, with her husband John, formally adopted Fatima when she was 14. Fatima finally had a real family.

In 1980, Whitbread competed in her first Olympic Games in Moscow, together with Commonwealth record holder, Tessa Sanderson, yet both failed to reach the final. In 1982 at the Commonwealth Games in Brisbane Fatima won a bronze medal and made a significant breakthrough in 1983, defeating Sanderson for the first time as well as improving her personal best to 69.54m.

At the 1983 World Championships in Helsinki, she only just made the final, qualifying in the twelfth and last position. However, in the final Fatima threw 69.14m in the first round, putting her in gold medal position until, in the very last round, home favourite Tina Lilak of Finland bettered 70m to relegate Fatima to silver medal, in front of an ecstatic home crowd.

Fatima's rivalry with Tessa Sanderson is by now legendary, and there certainly was no love lost between the two during their many confrontations during the 1980s. The middle distance events had Coe and Ovett, women's javelin had Tessa and Fatima, which served to raise the profile of the two throwers and just as significantly the profile of the event itself. Crowds all over Europe and beyond were entertained as they battled each other as well as with competitors such as Tina Lilak. Fatima's wink to camera and the famous 'Whitbread wiggle' became her trade mark for that era.

Her Commonwealth Games medals came in Brisbane in 1982 where she ended with a bronze by losing out to Sue Howland and Petra Rivers of Australia; and silver in 1986, in Edinburgh where she was disappointed to finish behind Tessa Sanderson.

Fatima competed in three Olympics, winning bronze at the 1984 Los Angeles games, where Tessa won gold, and silver in 1988 at Seoul, where Petra Felke won gold.

Head to head rivalry throws up fascinating circumstances; having lost out to Tessa in Los Angeles in 1984, Fatima went on to beat Tessa in seven straight competitions. She then lost out to Tessa yet again at the 1986 Commonwealth Games. At one stage five of the six longest throws by a woman were by Fatima. In the mid eighties Petra Felke went through a dominant purple patch where she only lost three times – each time to Fatima.

However in 1986 at the European Championships, early one morning during the qualifying round, with few people, or members of the press for that matter, present in the stadium, she set a stunning new world record, beating Petra Felke's old record by two metres. She was crowned European Champion and the new World Record holder, in what was to be her finest athletic moment. Fatima went to Rome for the 1997 World Championships where she upstaged everyone and took the title with a throw of 76.64m a new Championship Record. After an enthralling battle Petra Felke finished 5 metres behind Fatima in second place.

Fatima's career was cut short by a serious shoulder injury, which also brought to an end the era when two British rivals took hold of the javelin event – and gave it a damn good shaking.

Fatima married her long term partner Andy Norman, who sadly passed away in 2007.

Fatima has a beautiful son Ryan, who is her pride and joy.

Kriss Akabusi

"Bang!! Boom!! Feeoo, feeoo, feeoo, Bosh! That was it."

Kriss Kezie Uche Chukwu Duru Akabusi is a flamboyant name for a flamboyant man, but if the first thing that comes to your mind is 'Awight' or 'Pump it up' or 'Awoooooga!' [or was that John Fashanu's catchphrase?] then we are not thinking of the same man. OK even before his TV career, Kriss was always a larger than life character. When he was in the room you certainly knew he was there, usually in a shiny shell suit or a crazy jumper! He may have been the court jester – but he was not to be taken as a joke.

Even if you had finished last in a race, Kriss would always be able to bring you around. He had an infectious laugh, and would be able to bring you back to reality. He puts athletics in its right place, in your life. It's a very short part of your life and he makes you realise it's not life or death, and he does it without disrespecting your will to win – but he brings it home. He makes you get over a disappointment, re-group, move on and ensure the next time – you deliver.

On the track his was a story of reinvention, a change from one event to another, a feat not attempted by many and accomplished successfully by few. He was a rare breed, a seemingly raw and precocious athlete with an abundance of energy which always threatened to take him to the top of something.

For me, his time finally came, on the 1st of September 1991 at the World Championships in Tokyo. I thought he might remember it of sorts!

CJ: This sure is a beautiful day here in . . .

KA: In good old London town, how are you Colin me old mucker. Good to see you brother.

CJ: Good to see you too, looking sharp. I like the cloth!

KA: Not bad is it! It's good to be here with you me old buddy, we go back a long way, a long way.

CJ: We certainly do and I always had admiration for how you changed event, because you became a successful 400m runner, then ended up doing the 400m hurdles!

KA: It was a real challenge to be honest Colin, yes I started off as a quarter miler, a 400m runner, back in the mid 1980s, and I went to the very first World Championships in Helsinki as a reserve and got the taste for it. Then I went to the Los Angeles Olympics in 1984 and came home with a silver medal, but then a new generation of British athletes emerged – so I have you to blame for the change brother.

CJ: That's cool with me!

KA: In 1985 along came a guy called Roger Black, or Roger 'pretty boy' Black, and what I suddenly found was that I was going to the 1986 European Championships as baggage man!

CJ: Oh dear, not good Kriss.

KA: Not good at all Colin. Having been the best in the country, having been maybe the best quarter miler in Europe in 1984/85 here I was not good enough to get into the British team for the 4 x 400 metre relay. That was very hard to accept. Roger Black, Derek Redmond, Todd Bennett and Phil Brown were the guys in form and I was on the fringe. Not a happy bunny!

CJ: No I can imagine!

KA: So I was on the plane to Stuttgart with all this going on inside my head, and it was at that moment that I decided. NO! No way, I am no longer going to be a spectator here, I want my own event. I did run in the relay in the end through default as Todd Bennett and Phil Brown got injured, but my mind was made up. So after the Championships I looked at the British results. Right I thought, first the 800m, some guy called Seb Coe won that with Tom McKean second and Steve Cram third, so I can forget the 800m I thought. Then I looked at the 400m hurdles results, and I saw not one of the Brits had got through the first round! Guess what. I am going to be a hurdler! Yiipppeee!!!

CJ: Amazing! But coming from a hurdle background myself – you were not a pretty hurdler Kriss.

KA: Well I am not the prettiest guy so that follows. I didn't want to run pretty Colin. You can run pretty and come in last; I wanted to win semi finals and make finals and stand a chance of winning a bit of metal mate. Now my PB as a quarter miler was 44.93s.

CJ: Yes set at the AAA's Championships when you beat all the best 400m runners in the UK, including Derek Redmond!

KA: I am humbled that you know that fact Colin, you should be doing TV commentary on athletics! Now as a hurdler my PB was 47.93s so I only had a differential of three seconds, so I must have been a reasonable hurdler, or at least an efficient one.

CJ: Under those circumstances that change must have been difficult?

KA: It was yes. I remember my first hurdle race and the commentator said 'Kris Akabusi runs like a wallowing rhino'. It didn't help having all my hurdles flying back into my face as I knocked them over left, right and centre! I then decided to try and knock them into my opponent's lane!

CJ: I never thought of that.

KA: I was enthusiastic, energetic and most certainly determined!

CJ: You became European Champion, Commonwealth Champion and medalled at the Olympics and at the World Championships – as a hurdler. That most definitely is success in anyone's book.

KA: Yes but do you know what I am most proud of as a hurdler – that I still hold the British record, as of today September 2010. Now your Welshman Dai Greene is getting close to it, but it has lasted for about twenty years so I must have been all right! Although I must be grateful you didn't take up the 400 hurdles and stuck at the 110 metre ones!

CJ: Oh no way could I have done that! I was chuffed to see your success, after being forced out of the 400m event, I remember thinking that you gave inspiration to people who needed to make a fresh start, and be as good as they had been in some previous role. But . . . .

KA: Ohhhh I love that, BUT, it sounded like a very positive and uplifting BUT . . . ?

CJ: Yes it is going to be. But – for me the most uplifting performance I saw was that of the 4 x 400 metre British relay team that won gold at the World Championships in Tokyo in 1991 by beating the American dream team! Now if a team were ever sprinkled with star dust it was you four.

KA: Oh Colin I love that. Sprinkled with star dust, dream dust, magic dust – it was a phenomenal moment really and even if I say it, a historic moment in British and World athletics.

CJ: I agree. I don't suppose you remember much about it do you Kriss . . . ?

KA: Colin, I do! There was a formula, a tried and tested way to run a 4 x 400 metre relay race. Everyone used it, no-one thought about it, which was basically that you put your best man on the last anchor leg, you put your second best man on the first leg, and the rubbish goes in the middle!

CJ: Right!

KA: Understand?

CJ: Yes. Where were you?

KA: In the middle, always!

CJ: Hahahha.

KA: So no-one really thought about changing the tried and tested. But we did. We were first and foremost great friends: Roger Black; Derek Redmond; John Regis – and myself, and we looked at the US team we were to face in the World final that day and came up with the idea of what we had to do if we wanted to 'hang out' with the best relay team in the world, and they were that, no question. We had to use a bit of nous. Being traditional would not get us the result we wanted so we thought it through.

We put our best man Roger 'pretty boy' Black on the first leg, so we could be up there at the end of the first lap. Then we would go with our second best man Derek 'Captain Courageous' Redmond, our only other 400m specialist, on the second leg. We hoped they could keep us up there for half the race, we hoped we might still be in contention at the 800 metres mark. Then John Regis, an out and out 200m runner goes on the third lap, so we would be competitive till the 1000 metre mark. So from then on it would be an unknown quantity because if John started to get lactic with 200m to go, we knew we would be in trouble before the old man Akabusi got the baton on the last leg. So that was our plan. We were to take on the mighty Americans and attack from the word GO!

CJ: When did people get to know about the changes?

KA: Well we announced the team an hour before the race, but when we went to the track side the Americans looked a little confused as they realised what we had done, but they certainly didn't look at all worried. David Coleman who was on TV commentary was going ballistic 'What's going on here, what are the British team up to . . . ' and all that. On the first leg for the Americans was Andrew Valmon, Pan American Champion and, unexpectedly, against him was 'pretty boy Black'.

BANG!! the gun goes and 'pretty boy' is out of his blocks and into that beautiful loping long stride pattern, hair perfect as he glides down the back straight and with a powerful display he hands over the baton ahead of Valmon, to Captain Courageous. But the Americans aren't that bothered because on the last lap they have their secret weapon.

So off goes injury prone Captain Courageous, he had only been training for the last six weeks due to injury – HANG ON IN THERE BIG GUY! He is up against Quincy Watts who the following year was to become the Olympic Champion, a hugely talented guy, brilliant athlete. The Captain runs the race of his life, and doesn't get injured. He is in the lead and Quincy is there at his shoulder trying to hang on, and into the home straight Quincy just goes passed him, but we are level pegging with the almighty American quartet.

Now over the baton goes to 'Johnny two chests' who runs against Danny Everett. Now Everett is slight as a stick, glides along like a smooth mountain spring, majestic. And pursuing him is the double barrel chested Regis who doesn't normally run the 400 metres unless you chuck him a few bob extra. Two chests is on the trail of the elegant Everett, John is working hard, big V chest, little ears, head back, two flaring nostrils, can he hold on for the last 200 of his lap? He is on the jock strap of Everett hanging on in there when suddenly it begins to happen, and the lactic is flowing. Oh my word he is looking ugly, he's caught a fridge, he has the monkey on his back, arms all over the shop, nostrils flaring, head back but still he hangs on in there and delivers the baton to me just two yards down on Everett. Phenomenal stuff and it was now over to Akabusi.

You mentioned star dust or magic dust Colin, and you know, I believe it had been sprinkled over the whole event. It was now old man Akabusi, I was a hurdler!!!!! – taking on Antonio Pettigrew, he was the Championship's individual 400 metre champion in a time of 44.57s. It was a mismatch – on paper.

The rest of the teams were well down the field, it was just him against me, the US against Britain, and in my mind we were just jogging.

It was a moment when I felt larger than large, time stood still, it was effortless, and it was like slow motion. I actually looked up at the stadium screen and saw us both alone there on the rack, and I just thought OK I will just keep up this jogging pace! Down the back straight we went and as we go into the bend I suddenly am presented with my opportunity as the pace seemed to drop just slightly as, I think, he prepared to wrap it up out of that bend. So I get him early. BOSH!! I am out of that curve into the home straight, and he is right there behind me, I can hear his turbo charger firing. BOOM!!

I can hear the noise of the baton swinging in his hand FOO, FOO, FOO as he gets closer, HE'S COMING!! Hang on in there; hang on in there, the ground is moving slower and slower under my feet, I am gasping for the line and for oxygen. BOOM!! I cross the line first, the crowd go mad, the team go mad, and the photographers go mad, Coleman on TV goes mad. The four Americans do not go mad, they just look stunned. For the first time in our lives we had beaten the mighty Americans on a World stage. Now that was magic!

CJ: Sensational, I have got goose bumps! I haven't spoken for ten minutes!

KA: Colin it was one of those defining moments in my life. Athletics is so often about the individual, but that day to be part of something greater, to be part of that team was one of the greatest moments of my life. When I see it on TV it's like watching someone else, like an out of body experience. It was great theatre and it was awesome to actually be at the top of something.

A guy called Aristotle said once that 'The team as a whole is greater than the sum of all its individual parts' and that is the only way I have to explain what we did that day. We beat four Americans who were individually better than us in every single way. I felt privileged that day to have come close to the ranks of British athletes like yourself, to feel a part of that generation of British athletes who set the public's minds alight during the 1980s and 1990s in track and field athletics.

CJ: Nice one brother, good to see you again.

KA: Good to see you too.

Kriss Akabusi MBE

Medals at major championships

Olympic Games

SILVER	1984	Los Angeles	4 x 400m relay
BRONZE	1992	Barcelona	400 mH
BRONZE	1992	Barcelona	4 x 400m relay

World Championships

GOLD	1991	Tokyo	4 x 400m relay
SILVER	1987	Rome	4 x 400m relay
BRONZE	1991	Tokyo	400mH

European Championships

GOLD	1986	Stuttgart	4 x 400m relay
GOLD	1990	Split	400mH
GOLD	1990	Split	4 x 400m relay

Commonwealth Games for England

GOLD	1990	Auckland	400mH
GOLD	1986	Edinburgh	4 x 400m relay

Personal best

400m	44.93	1988
110mh	14.6	1989
400mH	47.82	1992

b. 28th November 1958. Paddington, London.

Kriss was brought up in a children's home and went from there straight into the Army at the age of 16. He joined the British Army in 1975 and had a successful career in the Royal Corps of Signals before switching to the Army Physical Training Corps in 1981. His final rank was that of Warrant Officer Class 2.

Kriss, then a former army PT instructor, moved to Locks Heath in the early 1980s to train with Southampton & Eastleigh AC, but followed his first coach Mike Smith when he headed up Team Solent.

His career began in earnest in 1983 and he was soon representing Britain at the 1984 Olympic Games in Los Angeles. He was a member of the 4x400 metre relay squad that came home with silver, a squad made up of Kriss, Garry Cook, Phil Brown and Todd Bennett. The American team won.

His involvement in the Commonwealth Games of 1986, proved to be a life changing experience with him finding his faith. On the track the relay squad of Kriss, Phil Brown, Roger Black and Todd Bennett came home with gold medals and a time of 3.07.19s. He managed fourth place in the 400m sprint.

Further success followed for Kriss, again with the relay squad, at the World Championships of 1987 in Rome where, with Derek Redmond replacing Todd Bennett they won silver in a new area record time of 2.58.86s. The American team won with a new Championship record time of 2.57.29s.

By 1987 Kriss had switched from the 400m sprint event to the 400m hurdles and soon success came his way at the Commonwealth Games of 1990 where he won gold in a time of 48.89s. In the same year he won gold at the European Championships in a time of 47.92s beating David Hemery's 22-year-old British record, which had stood since the Olympics of 1968.

At those championships as part of the relay squad he picked up his second gold medal along with Roger Black, John Regis and Paul Sanders – in a European record time of 2.58.22s.

Kriss is best remembered for helping Britain clinch the gold medal, and beating the American team in the World Championship 4x400 metre relay in Tokyo in 1991. The quartet of Roger Black, Derek Redmond, John Regis and Kriss bucked the trend that had seen Britain competing for the silver behind the US team, and took them apart with a cunning plan that saw them switch the order of the British team. Their winning time was a new area record of 2.57.53s, beating the US team by four hundredths of a second.

It was their finest hour. Kriss also managed a bronze in his individual 400mH event breaking his own British record twice in the process and lowering it to 47.86s in the final.

The Barcelona Olympics of 1992 held high hopes for the British relay squad as well as for Kriss in the individual 400mH event. However he had to settle for a bronze medal in 47.82s but again smashing his own British record. The hopes of taking on the US relay team did not materialise and the British team came home third in 2.59.73s, behind the US and the Cuban teams.

To date this British 400mH record still stands today.

Having retired from athletics Kriss went on to become a TV presenter with a stint on the Big Breakfast, and co-hosted the BBC's Record Breakers programme.

Kriss now has his own corporate communications and training company and is renowned for his unique, and effective, style of motivational speaking.

www.akabusi.com

Steve Backley

"Even blind squirrels find an acorn now and again."

Steve was the baby member of the British team, younger than us, and he was the most successful of us all. The best javelin throwers in the world were European, so Steve never had an easy competition! Most of us could take it easy and avoid the big guns in say a European Championship. But not Steve! What he produced was just outstanding. Remember he was a world record holder from the age of 20 in 1989, and won his last European Championship title in 2002. Outstanding!

When he first came on the scene he was very naïve, and that made us giggle because we had been on the team for a few years. Steve came to my home city, Cardiff in 1990 and won the AAA Championships. We had a real good time and he threw around 88m. I am proud that he holds the stadium record.

As I drove into the 'London Golf Club' I think I spotted Steve on the practice range, and that didn't surprise me. Steve was one of the most competitive people I ever met. He is King Competitive! It didn't matter that I had NEVER hit a golf ball in all my life! All the more reason for Steve to make sure he didn't lose against a rookie! His competitive spirit was a crucial element in his makeup and he used it well. To say that he hated losing is such a great understatement. We all hated losing, the sport is so tough that losing hurts so bad. But with Steve I think it was on another level with him. Whatever you have in you – acknowledge it, develop it and utilise it to give you an edge over your opponents. It's not that they won't be competitive – they will. But there's being competitive – and then there's Mr. Steve Backley!

CJ: Well Steve you finally got me to a golf course!

SB: Yes finally after years of persuading! It makes me so happy because I remember a conversation we had a few years ago, about how you would never ever play a round of golf because you said you 'just didn't get it'. You know, golf spoils a good walk type of stuff! But here we are.

CJ: Ok tee me up – but I still 'don't get it'! What is this passion all about?

SB: This for me takes the place of athletics, or javelin throwing to be precise. You know when you finish competing, when you finish going to Olympic Games and World Championships and the rest of it, you retire and there is a huge hole. It is so hard to replace. But I found that I get a similar buzz from golf as I did from the javelin, you know the pressure, the competition – and certainly the banter. It's similar enough and I love it.

CJ: And the views here, and this countryside is so beautiful!

SB: Oh yes. OK just swing nice and easy and hit, let me stand back.

CJ: Am I holding this bat right?

SB: It's a club – and at least it's the right way up yes. Hold it with the right hand just as if you were shaking hands, and then the left hand just below the right, don't clasp it so tight, you aren't going to club someone – just a gentle grip – or that's what the pro told me.

CJ: OK here goes.

SB: Just let me move back a little more.

CJ: Crickey where did that go?

SB: Lucky for you it's just past the ladies tee. If it hadn't passed that you would be playing another with your trousers down. Yes that's golf mate, it's not a straightforward game at all. But, you got to be positive, at least you will find that one. Hit another.

CJ: Where did that one go?

SB: You got underneath that one, it's in the hedge over there, now we might not find that one. Here's another. Just let me make a phonecall to cancel a meeting I got later tonight mate.

CJ: Sorry?

SB: Nothing mate. You carry on.

CJ: OK. Here goes. Concentrate now CJ!

SB: Wow OK nice shot, middle of the fairway with a nice bounce, you are on your way. Five off the tee though.

CJ: Now that was pretty good.

SB: Yep, certainly was. Third time lucky for a Welshman, even a blind squirrel finds an acorn now and again.

CJ: I can see the attraction of being out here as early as this in the morning.

SB: Well you see the thing with javelin and golf is there are so many similarities and I get javelin thoughts when I hit golf balls. I love to see things fly a long way, it's in my blood, I can't help it. I've got this big ego thing going on, and I have to fight not to strangle the club trying to hit it miles and miles, so I have to concentrate on slowing the swing down to a blur. Here goes. Please God let me hit it past Colin's ball.

CJ: Wow good shot. It's gone past mine a long way but you are in the rough on the right. Mind you could break that club hitting the ground like that.

SB: Hahaha. I've sliced it into the rough, but no matter. It doesn't matter how you play it's just good to be out here.

CJ: Not sure if I believe you mate, but it is great walking down this quiet fairway. So from javelin to golf?

SB: Well if you are competitive and on a golf course it helps, there will be times in a round when it's not going well and you have to battle and grind – and we have both been there in athletics terms. It's a test of character, and you find out just what you are made of. You could say all our athletic principles are there; making a plan, believing in yourself, preparing well and executing a plan. Most importantly you have to believe, that the next hole will be a birdie.

CJ: I don't believe in miracles!

SB: Well look at the situation here. You are in the middle of the fairway, I am in the rough down there. You will get to the green – sometime before sundown!

CJ: Well if I could throw the ball I would kick your ass!

SB: Mmmmmm fighting talk Mr. Jackson, I like that.

CJ: Something's never change.

SB: Well you know I was well into the whole battle of the competition arena. From my 20 years in sport I have collated what I learnt and called it PAC training. Power, agility and coordination which for me are the key elements for power sports, and sports where you need to move well. We don't use it to teach someone how to play tennis but we do use it to teach tennis players how to be at their best to then play tennis. OK. You are 200m from the pin, nice easy swing again.

CJ: Here goes.

SB: You may need a few of us to help you carry that divot back up here! You are in the Mary Rand.

CJ: In the sand right?

SB: No sand left actually.

CJ: So you talked about preparation earlier.

SB: Yes you know you obviously have to prepare your body to be able to do what your event demands, but the basis of the PAC training schedules is to make a positive difference to improve people's ability in playing their sport. It's not just for javelin throwers.

CJ: If I was a young javelin thrower I would be straight on that web site!

SB: Well yes there is that, but we do try and make a difference across all sports as well as for those who coach, and that's what the role of a coach is – to make a difference. I started out as a cross country runner and middle distance runner, but it didn't feel right, and when I got into javelin I thought wow – this is for me. I was helped by some great East and West European coaches who enabled me to develop the buzz and enjoyment I got from javelin, and the help and advice and schedules that I was exposed to, made me into a fairly successful thrower.

CJ: Fairly successful yes four European titles, three Commonwealth titles and medalled at three Olympics. Not bad!

SB: Yes and I wouldn't have achieved any of that if I didn't understand how to prepare my body. First of all it's about understanding what will be required, then knowing how to work on specifics and then how to maintain your body's ability to perform. One unique area in particular for any athlete is how to rehab after injury. That has got to be right, so we have designed schedules for a huge range of situations and the response we get suggests what we are suggesting is right for many people. You will need the sand wedge.

CJ: Thanks. I hear what you are saying, and when that knowledge comes from someone with your record, from someone who has lived and breathed it – and got success from it then its worth something. In any walk of life, outside sport, it's like recognising what you haven't got, what you don't know, what you need – and then being proactive in acquiring those. Nice swing now Colin.

SB: Whoops. You can take a shower to get the sand out of your hair later. Try again. OK well in golf they would say that was an Arthur Scargill, and if I kick your ball just a little, there you are, you're on the green with a Dennis Wise of a putt.

CJ: What are you on about?

SB: Well an Arthur Scargill out of the bunker – great strike but not a great outcome. Dennis Wise, a nasty little five footer . . . or so they tell me.

CJ: OK. You are one up.

SB: This next hole is nice and straight, but long so let's make sure we can walk down the middle of the fairway, together.

CJ: OK. Tee it up high for me.

SB: You sure you want the wood? OK. Then stay nice and relaxed, think rhythm and timing from your hurdling days. Head down and let your body feel relaxed.

CJ: Nice and easy. Concentrate now CJ. Nice and easy and relaxed.

SB: Oh my word! Colin Jackson that shot is enormous! You are an absolute bandit. You scoundrel. That is a disgrace! That's 350 yards and more. Unbelievable!

CJ: That was incredible, I just swung . . . I don't know what . . . it's on the edge of the green. Wow what a feeling – now I am hooked!!

SB: Do you want to buy that driver off me?

CJ: That was an incredible feeling mate! Wow! What did I do right?

SB: Don't even analyse it, just feel that buzz! Enjoy it while it lasts.

CJ: Where's my putter so I can carry it down the fairway! Hey where you going?

SB: Hahahahaha . . . you bandit! I don't think I will dare play a shot here. I am going back to the buggy!

CJ: What!?

SB: Joking mate, just changing club having seen that. Let me introduce you to 'Big Bertha'!

CJ: Now that is one heck of a weight on that there Steve.

SB: Big Bertha named after the German Big Bertha Howitzer!

CJ: Did she throw javelin?

SB: I've got to get it past your ball Colin, I just got to. Sorry mate! This is pressure man. Hang on let me use one of my best balls too. Pressure, pressure, I can't believe this.

CJ: Hey no worries mate. I will just sit here. What you looking for?

SB: No just looking, uhh . . . I got bunkers right . . . and left. Your ball . . . lid in . . . between them to the green . . . If I can draw it round . . . maybe . . . or . . . go over the right . . . .

CJ: Is there a shop I am getting rather thirsty, I could do with a newspaper and . . . .

SB: Shut it Jackson, people know I am here with you, they will ask how the round went . . . .

CJ: Gee that was an enormous practice swing Steve. Will your feet be off the ground when you hit this one?

SB: See this is the feeling that I kind of love and hate all at the same time. Nothing personal mate but I do 'play golf', so I am expected to be able to do certain things and golf can be such a cruel game. As we found in athletics Colin, expectation can ruin the enjoyment, unless you learn to manage it. Your biggest competitor in golf is yourself. Dig deep Backley! Come on baby.

CJ: Oh my word. You did it. That shot is enormous.

SB: That is! Get up there.

CJ: Wow. They are very close together!

SB: Yes they are. If yours is furthest I am still giving up golf. First time on a course – you are having a laugh!

CJ: Still competitive Mr. Backley?

SB: Old habits – don't die!

CJ: Grab your putter and let's stroll. Like when you hit a home run. I like this! You were very young when you had success as a junior and your first World Record came along shortly after, how did you maintain your enthusiasm and your standards?

SB: I think it helped that all the best javelin throwers were European so I was always up against the best in any competition. I am very competitive, and when I went into battle against say Jan Zelezny, I just found it exhilarating to be head to toe with him. Just bring it on mate! Bring it on! We brought the best out of each other and we were good friends as well! I loved throwing the javelin, so keeping sharp and hungry for it was never a problem for me. The appeal was always to throw that thing as far as I could and to see it flying was a fantastic feeling.

CJ: You were breaking world records and a real household name in the UK.

SB: Yes the support British athletics had then was quite phenomenal across most of the track and field events, I think the British public were very knowledgeable about athletics then, and to be able to compete in that sort of environment really brought my competitive spirit alive. I also miss the laughs we had, and the tight group that were in the British team in those days.

CJ: I can understand that, so you must miss that opportunity to perform and to be in competition?

SB: Yes I do. I don't miss the injuries, but yes I miss the competitions and I miss the Union Jack going up the flag pole at a javelin medal ceremony! It would be so good to see that sight again. But golf is a great game, and it's good for me in lots of ways. Any golfer reading this bit will know what we are both feeling right now. Enjoy it – it may not last long! You will have to have a handicap rating if we play again!

CJ: What is a handicap?

SB: Don't worry about it, there are some very experienced golfers, who have been playing for years who still don't know what a handicap is.

CJ: Uhh? You beat me by a yard.

SB: But they are two fantastic drives mate. They really are. Fantastic! Well done Colin great shot. Now we need to at least make par. Come on Colin – put it in the hole.

CJ: No pressure!

SB: Ohhh . . . inches from it mate. That's a gimme, take it away. Birdie.

CJ: Ohhh . . . Hey yours will drop if you jump up and down!

SB: So close. Birdie as well, golf can be a kind game too – two birdies that's fair! Shake hands mate.

CJ: Blind squirrels do sometimes find acorns!

SB: Let's go find the 19th hole, see if we can get you to spend some money after that shot.

CJ: Well the tee for the 19th should be after the 18th green right?

SB: Aye aye. Bring your wallet Colin.

Steve Backley OBE

Medals at major championships

Olympic Games

SILVER	1996	Atlanta	Javelin
SILVER	2000	Sydney	Javelin
BRONZE	1992	Barcelona	Javelin

World Championships

SILVER	1995	Gothenburg	Javelin
SILVER	1997	Athens	Javelin

European Championships

GOLD	1990	Split	Javelin
GOLD	1994	Helsinki	Javelin
GOLD	1998	Budapest	Javelin
GOLD	2002	Munich	Javelin

Commonwealth Games for England

GOLD	1990	Auckland	Javelin
GOLD	1994	Victoria	Javelin
GOLD	2002	Manchester	Javelin
SILVER	1998	Kuala Lumpar	Javelin

Personal best

Javelin	91.46	1992

b. 12th February 1969. Sidcup. England.

Steve Backley starting out as a cross-country, and middle distance runner, before applying his talent to the javelin. He made an immediate impact by winning the European junior championships in Birmingham in 1987, and the following year set a new world junior record of 79.50m. He soon became the first Brit ever to hold the world number one title.

Steve finished his career with a remarkable haul of medals and titles including four European titles and three Commonwealth Games titles and was one of the most consistent performers in the British team for well over a decade. He was ranked number one in the world on three occasions and has held the world record three times.

In 1990 he was voted IAAF athlete of the year, and his performances that year included the first ever world record in a throwing discipline for a Brit. It came in Stockholm with an 89.58m throw that smashed the record of 89.10m. This feat put Steve into the elite band of world class athletes who were emerging in Britain during that era. Jan Zelezny of the Czech Republic bettered the record shortly after with 89.66m, but back came Steve with a huge 90.98m throw in front of his home supporters at Crystal Palace. Never before had the British public been so interested and enthralled by the javelin competition! A gold medal followed at the Auckland Commonwealth Games as well as gold at the European Championships in Split. Despite being injured for much of 1991 he still managed to entertain the crowd in Sheffield with a new British and Commonwealth record of 91.36m, and when the new javelin specifications were introduced in 1992 he threw it to a new world record distance of 91.46m in New Zealand.

His career pitted him against the best of the Scandinavian throwers where javelin throwing is a part of their sporting culture. Seppo Raty and Aki Parviainnen, as well as of course the legendary Jan Zelezny were Steve's great rivals and their battles defined the javelin competition for that era, as they traded titles and records.

At the 1992 Olympic Games in Barcelona he was outgunned by Zelezney who threw a new Olympic record to win gold, with Seppo Raty in second place and Steve taking home bronze.

In 1996 the Olympic dream continued in Atlanta, where the medals were again shared but in a different order with Zelezny again taking gold, Steve silver and Raty bronze. His pursuit of Olympic gold continued in 2000 at Sydney, during a season when he was recovering after knee surgery. Steve threw a new Olympic record of 89.95m, which looked like winning him the gold medal. However Jan Zelezny threw a third round 90.17m, which proved enough to sneak the gold medal and leave Steve in silver position.

His record fourth Olympic appearance for the British team came in 2004 at the Athens Games. A true competitor he threw a season's best of 84.13m, but it was only enough to secure fourth place – the gold went to a young man by the name of Andreas Thorkildsen of Norway. The King is dead, long live the King.

Steve was the first Brit to win four European titles; Split, Helsinki, Budapest and Munich, and these are evidence of his dominance. The fact that he was the first Brit, in any track and field event, to medal at three Olympic Games is evidence of his world class status.

Steve is a regular commentator on BBC Radio 5, and has various business and motivational speaker roles.

www.backleyblack.com

David Hemery

"Like running up sand dunes – the less effort you put in the harder it is."

David arranged for us to meet in a restaurant for a snack. He ordered a simple sandwich and an orange juice. Still slight of build, dignified, and with an endearing mannerism that immediately made me think of athletics in an era where there were very few 'frills.'

To me David was Mr. Perfection. He knew his event inside out and it was all about rhythm. Like the rhythm of a dance. Even if he didn't genuinely achieve perfection, his aura and his persona gave off the impression that he was just perfect. He was someone I would aspire to be like, because I liked attempting to achieve perfection.

The rewards in David's day certainly were not financial – athletics was still in its commercial infancy. However to call it the amateur or Corinthian era risks undermining the dedication David Hemery applied to the 400 metre hurdles, which I consider to be one of, if not the hardest and toughest event – and believe me they are all tough!

Sitting next to David I was aware that I was in the company of greatness, a man who defined British athletics, a real gentleman of British Sport. He had just come from a meeting about his Olympic legacy project called the 21st Century Legacy, and he was still fired up about it. His personal journey really did exemplify the correct way to do things, the correct way to conduct oneself, and I was interested in finding out what athletics brought to him personally.

CJ: David thank you for agreeing to meet up for a chat

DH: It's an absolute pleasure Colin, I love catching up and we don't do it often enough. I wanted to ask your advice – I am working on a project aimed at inspiring children called the 21st Century Legacy project and we are in the middle of trying to secure a financial partner at the moment – perhaps you have some ideas?

CJ: If I can help I will. You David were a 20th Century athlete and if I may, I would like to take you back to your gold medal performance at the Mexico City Olympics in 1968, because, to me, your win, really was the start of athletics in the psyche of the British public.

DH: Well it might well have been, because that was the first live Olympics on TV. The pictures were beamed over on what was then Telstar – on satellites that had just been put up, and for vast numbers of people that race was one of the first athletics events they would have seen on their black and white sets here in Britain. Now that does make me feel old! I suppose we were one of the first sporting events to be given the Telstar treatment. They were the Games where Bob Beamon jumped an enormous distance of 8.9m in the long jump, a record that stood till 1991, and where Dick Fosbury won gold with his Fosbury Flop technique, and I don't know if you knew this Colin but we had the first disqualification on the basis of a failed dope test.

CJ: No I didn't know that!

DH: Yes a Swedish pentathlete failed a drugs test – for alcohol! He must have drunk a fair few pints before competing! So the whole Olympic event, the whole experience was brought right into people's homes and into people's lives – and that is what sport does so well, so often in modern times.

CJ: Your performance was the only British success at those Games – and what a performance it was. If you had to write a script for that, so that it was imprinted in the minds of a UK audience, then you couldn't have written it better. Not only did you win gold, but you set a new world record. Surely you couldn't have foreseen that?

DH: It was my intention to run a time of 48.4s, which at the time was over half a second inside the World Record.

CJ: Wow!

DH: Yes, and the fact that I ran 48.12s was just an even bigger bonus! I mean aiming to break a world record is one thing but the margin of the victory came as a pleasant surprise and made it all the more memorable for people at home – as well as for David Coleman in the television commentary box. It's quite well known now that the race is also remembered for his faux pas of something like 'David Hemery wins for Britain, Hennige second – and frankly who cares who came third'. Well as it turned out Britain's John Sherwood cared very much who came third, because he did!

CJ: Coleman at his best! Now you took over half a second off the world record and it was the biggest winning margin for oh I don't know since, pre-history shall we say . . . because Germany's Gerhard Hennige was over a second behind you in second place, which equates to about 6 or 7 metres back on you. As an athlete I can appreciate that must have been a totally exciting experience for you.

DH: Oh it was, and I didn't imagine I would win by that distance, I thought that even if I was leading I may have others close to me, although it was a fast time. I had been through the race in my mind many, many times going into those games, and I dreamt about the final many times too! Athletics is like that, as you would know.

CJ: Yes I would dream about races as well the good ones and the not so good ones. Now I would describe you as having a flawless hurdling technique, on both legs.

DH: Oh no not at all!

CJ: Well I didn't expect you to say that!

DH: Well, no I didn't have a flawless technique – but I did have a technique, and I had great help from a chap who coached me Fred Housden. He worked on the simple observation that when you take a car from third gear to second gear you have to race the engine revs. So at the point where I was taking thirteen strides between hurdles and starting to fatigue, I would changed to fifteen strides but would crucially increase my speed of leg. It was such an advantage to be able to get that change right. In the first half of the race I would be able to take thirteen strides, an 8ft 6" stride, between hurdles comfortably, and when the body began to tire I had to do something which would compensate for the second half of the race.

CJ: Where did that hurdling technique come from then?

DH: Well believe it or not Colin, I started out in life as a high hurdler like you, not as good as you I hasten to add, but a high hurdler none the less, and that certainly gave me a good grounding as far as technique was concerned. I mean, many don't realise just how high those barriers are until you get up close to them, the margin for error is quite small. Would you not agree – here I am talking about your event!

CJ: Yes I certainly agree there's no better way to learn technique because if you clip one of those high hurdles not only does it hurt, but it puts you at the mercy of a terrific fall, and because you are travelling at such great speed you can end up in the next hurdle teeth first, head first or whatever first! You do not want to get high hurdling wrong – and you race at the very edge of that thin line of crashing out. I have often said that hurdling was the closest thing to flying, not only for the speed and the time you actually spend off the ground – but for that element of 'danger'.

DH: Yes, well it helped me a great deal, and yes hitting the high hurdles at pace sure could be a terrible experience, so I soon learnt to clear them too! I did win the 1970 Commonwealth Games title at the 110m hurdles, not a lot of people remember me for that!

CJ: I certainly do, Edinburgh, and you ran a very respectable 13.8 seconds.

DH: I did indeed young man! Nearly one second slower than your best. But when I realised, or my coaches realised, that I would be a better 400m hurdler – I then had to run a bend as well as clear the hurdles! OK the hurdles are lower in the 400m, we are not complete sadists! But running in lane eight was different to running in lane 1, so one race was never the same, you never stopped learning – or practising for that matter, because the event could bite you! I think perfection is unachievable to all intents and purposes, but to learn from the mistakes I made in a race, and to strive to better yourself to run the best you can is certainly achievable and that's what I always used to do.

CJ: Did you think that your World record would eventually be beaten by so much? I mean it's down now to sub 47 seconds.

DH: Well I knew I was not as fast as some sprinters, and certainly not as strong as some 400 metres runners who converted to the hurdles, like Kriss Akabusi who eventually took my British record, although we had to wait 22 years for that to happen. So I believe I did set a decent benchmark. But any world record, mine included, is just a stepping stone in an event, and it lasted four years before John Akii-Bua of Uganda broke it. But Colin, my time of 48.12 has stayed competitive, for example that would have won me a bronze medal in the Athens Olympics of 2004, and placed me just outside the bronze medal in Beijing 2008. So I do count it as a reasonably competitive time.

CJ: What did being an Olympian mean to you?

DH: That is a very difficult question to answer because that is very difficult to put into words. It's a very special experience being an Olympian, and an Olympic Games is a very special event to be part of, as a team member. It happened to be that both of our talents were in sport, and it epitomises what humans are capable of, if they integrate their body, mind, emotions and spirit. For me that was the essence. You can of course do that in other areas of life – however sport is a very public arena in which to perform, and an event like the Olympics enthralled an audience, so to be a winner under those circumstances was special and always will remain something quite special.

CJ: Who was your role model then?

DH: The very first role model I had was a British middle distance runner called Chris Chataway, and I remember being at the White City Stadium to see him beat Vladimir Kuts of the Soviet Union in an absolutely stunning race. That was in the same year as Roger Bannister's first sub 4 minute mile, in which Chris played a part. So it was a very inspirational year for many youngsters like me who had nothing much else to do in those days other than run and play outdoors – and it stuck in my memory certainly. I was at school at that time and we used to have a cross country handicapped race for all the pupils, whereby everyone was given a two second head start for every month they were younger than the oldest boy in the school, who started at the back. I was the youngest in the whole school and with that handicapped system I just managed to hold off the school's 18 yr old captain of athletics, to win the 3 mile race. Soon after that early show of promise, my Dad gave me a book all about Emil Zatopek a Czechoslovakian long-distance runner. He used to challenge himself in all sorts of ways like seeing how many telegraph poles he could run past whilst holding his breath. That book just inspired me to challenge myself in all sorts of situations to be the best I could. That was the catalyst not only to me in finding athletics, but also to guiding me to where I am today, in that I spent my adult life in education and inspiring youngsters is still a quest for me – a life quest.

CJ: That's what the 21st Century project is connected with?

DH: Yes for the past few years really I have been concentrating on this project which is intended to provide a catalyst for youngsters to want to become the best they can be, and to follow their dreams. We use Olympic athletes to inspire them whether that's in sport or in any other walk of life, to empower them to make choices and to try to be the best. That's true whether they want to be a hairdresser or a hurdler!

CJ: Do you think athletics can provide genuine role models?

DH: I am sure that sport in general can provide role models, and athletics is, I suppose, the most basic and fundamental of all sport, as everyone knows that running, jumping and throwing is involved in many other sports – so it is in a sense the underpinning purest side of endeavour. So certainly those who are the best in these areas can be tremendous role models – so long as they hold their integrity. That is the important part for me, it's not all about winning – it's also got to be about the way you win. I know you appreciate that Colin because I have heard you talk about that very point yourself, and of course you handled yourself in a way that you can be proud of.

CJ: I certainly agree its about how you win! Can I ask you what was the most memorable performance you ever witnessed in athletics?

DH: There were many memorable performances from many eras, but let me think, in terms of longevity, a guy called Alfred Adolf Oerter. He was an American discus thrower who won four successive Olympic gold medals – and in none of them was he the favourite. His career was very nearly over before it started as he had a very bad car accident in 1957. In one Olympics he slipped in the warm up throwing rink and broke a rib. But he just strapped up his ribs and continued throwing saying 'I haven't prepared this hard not to compete'. Everyone immediately wrote him off, but he delivered even under that pressure. I was fortunate to meet him some years ago and he said 'I still love to train – and if anything else good happens in the day then that's great!' So I think he was inspirational.

Also Ed Moses though, and the fact that for ten years he was undefeated, that is quite sensational. He is an exceptional role model for anyone. He respected every opponent and never took any race or any opponent for granted. His record is even more remarkable because, like you Colin, I believe you can learn more from a defeat than you can from a success. So for him not to experience defeat, in ten years, shows how much he learnt from each success. If we in this country could turn our win – lose mentality to a win – learn mentality, think how powerful that would be for everyone. If you don't take risks and get out of your comfort zone then you may never fulfil your potential.

CJ: I will never forget one of my early races where I lost, I came second, and the TV commentator said 'Jackson will never be a great hurdler because look, he is smiling and he only came second.' Now little did he know that although I was smiling – I was hurting so bad inside it was unreal. I smiled till I had shaken hands with the winner, and had got out of the arena. In the tears that followed, I promised myself I would never make the same mistakes again in a race.

DH: Yes well we so often forget to learn from our mistakes, and there is something you can take from every unsuccessful race, and if we don't do that in sport, or in life, then aren't we bound to carry on making the same mistakes over and over again? Efficiency is a good word.

CJ: What has athletics given you?

DH: I think athletics gave me a huge sense of self-understanding. There are so many levels to it, of self discovery. If someone had told me – when I was a seventeen year old running 53.5s for the 400m flat, that I would one day run 44.6s for a 400m relay leg, and 48.12s for the 400m hurdles, well I would have laughed at them. In order to do that I needed the assistance of coaches, but I needed to understand myself and what I was capable of. The mind and the body are powerful but only if you know and understand what's going on there.

CJ: Your family moved to the States when you were twelve years old, did that help progress you as an athlete?

DH: It may be unfair because I don't know how I would have developed had I not left Britain, but certainly racing on the US collegiate circuit provided me with a regular high standard of competition. I don't know whether I would have found that back here. The facilities were better in the US, for what they were at the time, and being coached by Billy Smith was integral. He put me through some of the most demanding training schedules imaginable, and he also understood me as a person as a human being and that was crucial if he were to succeed at coaching and helping me. Also the weather, if I remember correctly, wasn't British!

CJ: What do you define as success?

DH: It's the learning about oneself, and it's the setting of personal bests. That self improvement in your personal performance deserves and merits recognition. That deserves as much of a pat on the back as does the person who is capable of winning – and does so. I adored sand-dune running. It was totally exhausting. If you think about it you can only make progress up a sand dune by running flat out, that means there can be no short cuts. Try going slow and you don't make much ground. The less you put in, the harder it is, and the longer it takes to summit. So there is only one way to get better at running up sand dunes, and learning to deal with the associated pain is an important part of the self improvement.

CJ: What advice would you give to a young hurdler, struggling out there, with the ambition to improve?

DH: Well I will give a very practical answer. One simple exercise is to put a low level hurdle every other high hurdle, this means you can get your stride pattern going and work to get into the groove of your stride pattern. The lower hurdle will take a little pressure off while you work that stride pattern out. It worked well for me. For all youngsters in sport, I guess all I can say is one step at a time. Challenge yourself to improve. I remember vividly being aged nine or ten, just after Bannister's sub four minute mile run, and being out in the back garden of our home in Cirencester, running around like some fool, pretending that I was involved in some great race or other.

The old lady who lived next door with her thirty cats came out and shouted to me that I ran like Bannister, and I thought Wow, and I proceeded to run even harder! So she too was a catalyst for me. Find your own catalysts. You may wish to look to the performances of the past, and hear how champions became champions. However remember, at the end of the day, those champions are all human! Success doesn't just randomly happen to people. They make decisions and choices to improve and to attempt to become the best they can be. If that wins you a gold, or a record or an award then so be it. But if it doesn't then at the end of the day you can at least say I was the best I could be, because I gave it my full attention and effort. That in itself can be extremely rewarding. Great careers and performances, like your own Colin, should be an inspiration for young people, and when they have been achieved with dignity, like your own, there can be no limit to what others can draw from them.

I mean you must meet people all the time Colin who say to you 'you were my inspiration', and that is a terrific thing to hear.

CJ: I do get that, as many successful athletes do. I agree, as I also have my own sporting icons that have inspired me, because each has shown elements of what it takes to be great. They inspired me during my career, but also, since retiring I still look to their stories and take a piece of inspiration which will help me in life situations, whether that be doing Strictly Come Dancing, or to do with my business at Red Shoes. They are insights that you can pick out and keep with you.

DH: Absolutely. I also get people saying to me 'you were the first satellite sportsman'. Contemplate that one if you have time Colin!

CJ: I will indeed, well you were certainly a flier!

DH: Thanks I will take that as a compliment, from one flier to another.

David Hemery CBE

Medals at major championships

Olympic Games

GOLD	1968	Mexico City	400mH
SILVER	1972	Munich	4 x 400m relay
BRONZE	1972	Munich	400mH

Europeans

SILVER	1969	Athens	110mH

Commonwealth Games for England

GOLD	1966	Kingston	120 yH
GOLD	1970	Edinburgh	110mH

Personal bests

120yH	13.6	1969
110mH	13.72	1970
400mH	48.12	1968

b. 18 July 1944. Cirencester, Gloucester.

David Hemery was born in Britain yet his father's job as an accountant took the family to the US when he was twelve years old, where he continued with the early promise he showed as a youngster. British coach Fred Housden took him from a US High School best time of 16.5s for the 120 yds hurdles to a time of 14.7s which won David the AAA Junior championship title when he returned briefly, as an 18 year old to Britain, before resuming his studies in the US. It was in the States as a student at Boston University, Massachusetts that David worked to improve first of all as a sprint hurdler before switching to the longer 400mH distance, under the watchful eye and the careful guidance of Fred Smith.

David's first major title came in the 1966 Commonwealth Games in Kingston where he ran 14.1s for the then 120 yard hurdles. He was benefiting greatly from the US collegiate competitions where he had regular top class competition.

The Olympic Games of 1968 were the target for Team Hemery, but despite co-holding the Commonwealth and British records with John Sherwood at 49.3s they both were the slowest qualifiers for the final. A blistering performance by both men saw David win gold and John bronze, with David's winning margin the biggest since 1924. He ran ten British records during 1968, five at 440y hurdles and five more at 400mH, and his wining time at the Olympics stood as a British record for 22 years.

He retained his Commonwealth title four years later at the Edinburgh games, by then it was the 110m hurdles which he won in 13.6 seconds. In 1969, David won silver in 13.7s at the European Championships in Athens, Greece again in the 110m hurdles, behind Eddy Ottoz of Italy and ahead of Britain's Allan Pascoe. He did defend his 400mH Olympic title at Munich in1972, yet could only finish third, behind John Akii-Bua from Uganda, who set a new world record of 47.82s. David did take home two medals as he was a member of the silver medal winning 4x400m relay team. During his career David set six British records at 110m/120y hurdles with a best time of 13.6 in 1979. He also won the World Student Games in Turin in 1970.

After his running career, David worked as a coach in the United States and Great Britain. For a period in the 1970s he taught at the famous English school Millfield, and in 1998, he was elected as the first president of UK Athletics.

David won the first ever British Superstars competition, held in 1973, and followed it up with a second victory in 1976.

His current 21st Century Project is set to be one of the lasting legacies of the 2012 London Olympic Games.

www.21stcenturylegacy.com

THE MOSES PROJECT

Two schools 4,000 miles apart are at the centre of 'The Moses Project': Ysgol Iolo Morganwg, Cowbridge and Endonyiosidai School, Kenya. This international relationship is built around the correspondence between the children of these two schools, a correspondence which has far reaching educational and social benefits for all involved.

'The Moses Project' has been established to provide assistance for the Masai children whilst also encouraging an understanding of global citizenship and sustainability. The Project has already helped replace the original mud hut school for a larger, stone built construction and basic educational supplies have been collected by the children of Ysgol Iolo and sent out to the school in Endonyiosidai.

In response to the suggestions of the Masai children, and their inspirational volunteer teacher Moses, the exciting next chapter is underway: to provide a source of solar/wind energy which would enable power for lighting, a water pump and the means to cook a hot meal. The availability of renewable energy would encourage more Masai children to walk the long distances to school from their rural homes.

Despite the contrast in their day to day lives the children of both schools share the same dreams and have similar ambitions. Through this Project our children will be able to see how their ideas and actions can be life changing for their new friends in Kenya.

The Moses Project is supported by the 'Wales Africa Community Links' project, funded by the Welsh Assembly Government's 'Wales for Africa' scheme.

www.themosesproject.org.uk